Successful Reforestation in South Korea

Strong Leadership of Ex-President Park Chung-Hee

LEE KYUNG-JOON

Professor Emeritus,
Seoul National University, Seoul, Korea

"Republic of Korea is the only developing country that has succeeded in reforestation after the Second World War."

(from an UN FAO Report in 1982 titled "Village Forestry Development in the Republic of Korea")

"South Korea is in many ways a reforestation model for the rest of the world. .... It was gratifying for me to see the luxuriant stand of trees on mountains that a generation ago were bare. We can reforest the earth."

(from a book in 2006 titled "Plan B 2.0: Rescuing a Planet Under Stress and a Civilization in Trouble" by Lester R. Brown, Founder of Earth Policy Institute)

"I believe that only when dense forests which are a source of clean rivers and atmosphere are beautifully harmonized with a highly industrialized society can we enjoy a rich life in healthy and dignified spiritual culture."

(from New Year's Press Conference, January 1978 by President Park Chung-Hee, Republic of Korea)

Front Cover Photo:
President Park Chung-Hee embracing an Italian poplar tree planted in Dangjeong-ri, Dongbu-myeon, Gwangju-gun, Gyeonggi-do, ushered by Mr. Jang Gi-Yeong, the Deputy Prime Minister of Finance and Economy on March 6, 1966.

CONTENTS

Book Recommendation

Goh Kun (the 30th and 35th Prime Minister of the Republic of Korea, currently Honorary Chief Director of the Climate Change Center)

These days, we can see dense forests anywhere in the whole country. Strolling through the green forest, I sometimes recall the old past, giving myself to deep emotion. Until I reached my thirties, all the mountains at the backs of villages had been completely denuded.

At the beginning of the 1970s, I was devoting myself to my duties as a young deputy commissioner in charge of the Saemaul Movement in the Ministry of Home Affairs when I was given a special order to take on an erosion-control project on Mt. Dongdaebon on the border of Gyeongnam and Gyeongbuk Provinces. Mt. Dongdaebon is a large mountain located between Woidong-myeon in Weolsung-gun and Nongso-myeon in Uljoo-gun. One can catch sight of this mountain upon entering the airspace of our country by plane from Tokyo. Now it is green after the successful erosion control, but at that time it was a bald mountain. President Park Chung-Hee did not like the fact that this stripped mountain was the first sight in Korea to greet flying visitors who had just viewed the thickly forested mountains of Japan. As the Saemaul Movement director, I had the opportunity to command labor, take charge of reforestation, and successfully recover the hillside, in spite of difficult circumstances.

For this reason, I was entrusted in 1973 with a tremendous responsibility to set up the "First Ten-Year Forest Rehabilitation Plan." Although the responsibility originally rested on the Forest Service under the Ministry of Agriculture and Forestry, it fell on the Saemaul

Movement team after the recent transfer of Forest Service to the Ministry of Home Affairs. After spending day and night visiting mountain areas throughout the country for a couple of months, I was given the presidential order to report as a program planner in the relevant ministers' meeting.

In front of the president, I explained the three principles of national, fast, and economic reforestation. In an attempt to reforest the whole country within ten years, I introduced the concept of "national tree-planting" which involved participation of the whole nation through the Saemaul Movement. I emphasized "fast reforestation" in consideration of the urgency of repeated droughts, floods, and poor harvests in vicious cycles caused by the denuded mountains. I suggested both the selection of ten major tree species, and the planting of fast-growing trees and slow-growing timber trees with a ratio of seven to three. Also I proposed "economic reforestation" through the Saemaul tree nursery operation, a cooperative project between government and villages that would create the villages' common income while supplying forest fuel for village farmers. The content of the Ten-year Reforestation Plan reported on this day was determined as a state policy right away.

The basic framework of the Ten-Year Reforestation Plan established this way proceeded smoothly in accordance with the detailed project plan of the Forest Service. In 1973, the Ten-Year Reforestation Plan, in conjunction with both the Saemaul Movement already initiated, with the whole nation's support, and the heavy chemical industry project recently enacted, were considered the three major state projects. The first ten-year reforestation project, with a plan to plant a total of 2.1 billion trees in a million hectares (ha) within ten years, was accomplished in only six years, while the second 10-year plan, starting in 1979, was also completed early in 1987, in just nine years, making the whole country covered with green mountains. In the next year, 1988, the attraction generated by the Seoul Olympic Games allowed the publicizing of Korea's successful reforestation to the whole world.

Through its 1982 official report, the Food and Agriculture Organization (FAO) under the UN extolled "Korea as the only developing country that has succeeded in reforestation since World War II." Korea's reforestation is now widely known in the field of restoring the environment as a miracle of the twentieth century. As the person in charge of establishing the initial plan of this historical reforestation project in the 1970s, I still take pride in it, feeling a great reward.

This book was written by Professor Emeritus, Lee Kyung-Joon at Seoul National University in a form that documented Korea's history of forest devastation and the process of the successful reforestation in the 1970s, with a focus on the roles of Ex-President Park Chung-Hee. It was initially published in Korean in 2010 with great reviews from experts, and I also read it after receiving the author's copy. To exclude any subjective interpretation on reforestation, it was said that the author wrote this book based on the Forestry Service's written records, objective data already published by other authors, and interviews with over twenty related figures. While excluding political interpretation, as intended by Professor Lee, this book is intended to remain as a historical record for posterity by its chronicling of the successful reforestation process in Korea in the twentieth century, together with descriptions of the economic and social circumstances in those days.

The publication of this book in English gives the author an opportunity to let the world know about Korea's successful reforestation. I expect that this book will be welcomed by readers who have an interest in Korea's economic development and miraculous forest recovery. Once again, I would like to congratulate the author on the publication of this English edition!

Book Recommendation
Remembering Why South Korea's Reforestation Movement under President Park Chung-Hee Was So Important

Kim Chung-Yum (Former Chief of Staff for President Park Chung-Hee and Current President of Park Chung-Hee Memorial and Library)

Today, South Korea and its many mountains are covered with lush trees and dense forests. But it was not always like this. Nearly half a century ago, the country's landscape was as barren and hopeless as was its economic future.

South Korea underwent rapid and sustained social economic transformation under President Park Chung-Hee, transitioning from a poor agrarian economy to an industrialized nation in a single generation. South Korea's rapid economic ascent was powered by an export-driven industrialization. Less known but just as important were the rural development policies of the 1970s that ensured Korea's prosperity was broadly shared by reducing poverty and improving standards of living in the rural regions. The Saemaul (New Village) Movement was at the heart of the government's rural policies. It was a movement to change the hearts and minds of South Korean farmers based on the principles of self-help and cooperation. One of the biggest accomplishments of the rural development policies, implemented along with the Saemaul (New Village), was the reforestation movement, which stands as one of South Korea's greatest achievements, alongside its industrialization.

Indeed, I saw with amazement at how South Korea's barren and empty landscape changed and regained life during my service in government and the Office of the President. The country went from being bare of any trees to being filled with tall trees and green vegetation, as far as the eye could see. It was as if a green blanket had covered the whole country almost overnight.

South Korea's reforestation was a massive effort on the part of the government and its people. A great deal of time and effort was spent on planning and implementing the reforestation policies and on mobilizing the resources of the government. Under the Ten-Year Forest Rehabilitation Plan, all levels of government, beginning from the top with President Park and the Office of the President in coordination with the Korea Forest Service under the Ministry of Home Affairs, and down to the local governments, were actively involved. Most importantly, it was the hard work of the people directly involved in carrying out the reforestation policies, and the participation of the farmers through the Saemaul Movement and of the entire country that made it possible. What was initially planned to take 10 years was accomplished in only six years, during which nearly 2.9 billion trees were planted, covering 1.08 million ha of land.

Many people have forgotten or are too young to remember that South Korea was once completely stripped of trees and vegetation merely 50 years ago, after years of deforestation and devastation. If it were not for the efforts of the government and its people forty years ago to rehabilitate and replant South Korea's landscape with trees, I would not dare to say that we would be enjoying the fruits of their labor today. This is why "Successful Reforestation in South Korea: Strong Leadership of Ex-President Park Chung-Hee" written by Dr. Lee Kyung-Joon, professor emeritus at Seoul National University, is so important to better understanding South Korea's economic development and history. The study of South Korea's reforestation efforts during the 1970s can serve as an important source of information and insight for scholars, students, and practitioners, in the fields of development, environmental conservation, and various disciplines of social studies. I also highly recommend his book for anyone who is interested in learning more about South Korea's rural development and the Saemaul Movement.

Foreword

These days, many countries of the world appear willing to make Korea an object of their study. It is because this country, which had been at the bottom of the list of most backward countries even until the beginning of the 1960s, has now become one of the top-ten global trading countries. But that's not all. Through the Saemaul (New Community) Movement, Korea has transformed into a country with surplus of staple food while, according to the Food and Agriculture Organization of the UN, winning accreditation in 1982 as "the only developing country that succeeded in reforestation after World War II". This accomplishment carries great significance. When a developing country has made an economic development, it also means that it has destroyed the environment. However, Korea is an exception from this common observation, for it is now one of the few countries that is moving forward with "Green growth". Several of these facts must account for the attention the country has recently been drawing.

Interestingly, in Korea, where all the mountains are covered with dense forest, many young generations in their twenties and thirties take it for granted that the country has been thickly forested from old times. In fact, people now in their fifties and older remember living through tormenting poverty and still vividly remember the picture of mountains disastrously and poorly clothed forty years ago. The landscape of South Korea half a century ago was no different from the current bald mountains of North Korea, which has been recently reported through media outlets off and on.

This book tells the story of Korea's successful reforestation. It deals with how the Korean people miraculously restored themselves in half a century following thirty-five years of Japanese rule at the beginning of the twentieth century, its exploitation of resources which resulted in extremely denuded forests, liberation of the country, and then the turmoil of the Korean War (1950-1953) with over 2.3 million casualties. Korea is a mostly mountainous country with many rough physical aspects. It was not possible for a few patriotic persons or private organizations to take the lead in reforesting such extensive areas occupying 66 percent of the total land area. Instead, with an iron will, the government came forward and executed this project.

This kind of strong will toward reforestation originated with the sovereign, President Park Chung-Hee. President Park put his heart and soul into reconstructing the backward economy. He did his best to revive the national economy by promoting exports using rich human resources because Korea had very limited natural resources. At the same time, President Park drove forward the project of reforestation with a firm faith and strong leadership. Despite insufficient national finances, he was determined to hand down a scenic land to the next generation, and encouraged and guided the whole nation to participate cooperatively in planting trees.

If not for the ruler's insight and faith, it is indeed in doubt whether Korea would have fulfilled its national reforestation. The reforestation project was possible at that time because there were many hungry farmers and abundant labor in the rural communities. After that time, however, mobilization of so much manpower for reforestation would have been almost impossible because of the decrease in rural population, aging of the population, a weakened cooperative spirit, and the rise in labor cost.

This book ignores discussions of President Park's political aspects, which could be controversial. Instead, the book is based solely on the objective data on national reforestation. The author referred to the records and testimonies by as many persons concerned as possible in order not to be too subjective. However, the author tried to describe the exact situations at that time, since social and economic circumstances in which national reforestation was driven forward could be an important standard of judgment.

The author wants to express his sincere appreciation to the Forest Service and Forestry Weekly News for providing some of the valuable pictures, and to the following persons for interviews with the author;

Park Jin-Hwan (former Presidential Secretary for Economics), Oh Whee-Young (former Presidential Secretary for Landscaping and Construction), Kim Young-Joon (former Minister of Agriculture and Forestry), Sohn Soo-Ik (former Head of Forest Service), Kim Yeon-Pyo (former Vice Head of Forest Service), Kim Gap-Seong (former Director of Forest Experiment Station), and Park Seung-Geol (former Director of Central Forest Experiment Station).

The author would like to express sincere appreciation to Goh Kun, former Prime Minister, and Kim Chung-Yum, former Chief of Staff for President Park Chung-Hee for writing the book recommendation, to Kim Euy-Chul for assistance in writing the Korean edition of this book, to his wife, Sung, for improving the quality of many pictures by Photoshop, and to his son, Joseph, for designing the book cover.

Prologue: A Poor Country

If we go back to 1960, this profile was widely possible about South Korea (the Republic of Korea): it was a country located on half of a small peninsula in the Far East. The country had fallen victim as a colony to a big power in the previous century, and after the World War II, it was invaded by the communists in the Korean War (1950-1953), which produced 2.3 million casualties and brought about utter ruin of the country. More importantly, South Korea was a poor country that seemed without any hope. Its population was 25 million as of 1960, with a high density of population (fourth in the world), and an annual population growth of 2.9 percent (sixth in the world).

Looking at the data of national income per capita for 1959 for 120 countries registered in the UN, the first rank was the US ($2,250) and second Canada ($1,521), followed by Sweden ($1,387), Switzerland ($1,299), the U.K. ($1,023) and West Germany ($833). Japan ($299) was twenty-fifth, and South Korea ($76) stood at 119th among the 120 countries, the lowest-ranked except for India. The Philippines ($170), Thailand ($220), as well as Greece, Turkey, South Africa and Colombia (all $200 to $400 level) were all higher than Korea.

In 1961, our country exported US $40.8 million of goods and imported $316 million. It was a miserable record. The Gross National Product was $2.1 billion, and its harvest of rice, the staple food, was 24 million 'seom' (3.46 million tons). Such an amount of rice was absolutely insufficient to support the domestic need, but buying it abroad was impossible due to the lack of foreign exchange. In 1960, the country barely survived by receiving economic aid of $240 million from overseas.

Photo 1. Mountains with only clumsy young trees sparsely scattered and a few sleepy thatched houses at the foot of the mountain. It's a picture of north Gyeonggi-do at the beginning of the 1960s.

Food and necessities were not all that was scarce. The country also had a severe lack of drinking water. Our country enjoys as much precipitation as any country of the world. But the falling rains only drained off of bald mountains without trees and pushed soil downward to sweep away houses, paddies, and dry fields. Mother Nature didn't bother to store up water, nor could we humans exercise wisdom in gathering water for use.

In Seoul, each house did have one faucet in the yard, but it was of no use at all for homes higher elevations. And even in low-lying areas, it wasn't possible to obtain several pails of water until midnight. Taking a shower at home as we do these days was unimaginable, because the minimum amount of water needed for bathing was not available. At that time the author was young and lived in Seoul. Residents living in little higher section in the neighborhood had to wait in line at a public water faucet every day for over an hour. They were able to obtain only two buckets of water to carry home on a yoke.

Failure to conserve rivers and forests does not presage just water shortage. It leads to a decrease in the rice crop. With rain, the rice paddy is overrun, and without rain it is cracked at the bottom, so rice plants cannot grow properly. Does this hold true for rice plants only? All living things from crops to vegetables, fruits, and even livestock, need water. Failure to conserve rivers and forests makes human living itself impossible. A desert is a good example.

To be used properly for man, water must go through two stages: suitable precipitation and wise management. While the former is God's jurisdiction, the latter is man's business. It is truly profound that even drinking a cup of water takes harmony between God and man. Management of water is also divided into two phases: storage and purification. Although the process of purifying water may be technologically manageable if there is water anyway, storage is another story because it is such a gigantic business. Storage of water is taken charge of by two main bodies. One is water-storing facilities, including a dam, and the other is a forest. From a mountain luxuriant with trees, clean water springs up all year round. The riverhead of large rivers is without exception "a small fountain in a deep mountain." All river waters flowing in torrents at the lower reaches begin by flowing, bit by bit, from springs in the forest.

Which has a larger water capacity a dam or a mountain? Which will be greater in storage capacity all of the dams or all of the mountains in our country? Korea is a mountainous country with mountain forests covering about 64% of the country. The total amount of water stored in the mountains is 18 billion tons. This amount is nine times as much as the 1.9 billion-ton effective storage of the Soyang River Dam, the largest domestic dam, and 4 billion tons greater than the total capacity of the 14 billion-ton (based on 2006 statistics) storage of forty-nine chief domestic dams. This great storage is possible because the mountains are thick with trees. In a place without trees, however, even if a dam has been built, water will not gather properly. More soil than water will soon be swept down to fill the dam, which is why trees and dams must go together.

Let's go back to 1960. At this time, the majority of the mountains in our country were bare ones, and there were only a few dams worthy of the name. Four dams, completed in the colonial days and the Goesan Dam built after the country's liberation, were all of them, and as for storage, except for the Hwacheon Dam (with a 660-million ton capacity), all were small dams under the 100-million ton level. This explains the water shortage mentioned earlier.

After that, the government pushed for building additional dams, until today we have a total of forty-nine major dams around the country, while reclaiming forests in upstream catchment areas and raising their storage capacity. As a result, in 1985 (the first year with official records), the supply of piped water in the city of Seoul was recorded at an annual 1.3 billion tons, enabling Seoul citizens to use water as they pleased. As of 2013, Seoul with a population of ten million people is supplying 3.4 million tons to its citizens each day. This means that one Seoul citizen is using 0.3 tons of water a day. This is how we now can run a washing machine as often as we need, the whole nation can take a shower at home every day, and industrial facilities can be built any place in the country without restraint. So where can this much water we are now using come from? It is true that precipitation has increased since 1961, but its increment is small. Then what is it that has allowed us to use water as we please? .

Photo 2. Mountains were also stripped near cities. Picture shows a desolate mountain around Donam-dong, the northern part of Seoul, at the beginning of the 1960s.

The author retired from a university, concluding forty years of life as a scientist in forestry. However, there is one thing left I have to do as a forestry expert to trace the process by which Korea has recovered its old picture of scenic beauty and to trace a person who specifically contributed to it. Another goal is to clarify that his secret of success was forest rehabilitation and to record the related tracks to hand them down to posterity.

Part 1.

At the Threshold of Desertification

Chapter 1. The Treeless Korean Peninsula

Causes of Devastated Mountain Forests

"It is surrounded by mountains with sparse shades of pine trees here and there but they are almost denuded." These words relate the first impression of Seoul by Isabella Bishop (1832-1904), a famous British geographer and travel writer. After visiting the Joseon Dynasty at the beginning of 1894, Bishop wrote a book titled <*Korea and Her Neighbors*>.

The observation was not concerning the area around Seoul only. A Russian Lieutenant Colonel Beverly, who traveled in Hambuk Province in 1889, wrote in his book <*Koree Puteshestbiia*>, "The forest has been completely destroyed here. It barely remains only in a secluded place in the mountains from which harvested timber was impossible to carry out." Homer B. Hulbert (1863-1949), an American missionary who remained with Joseon until the end of the Korean Empire, said in 1906 in his book <*The Passing of Korea*>, "No matter where we go in this peninsula, we can see bare mountains, which contrasts greatly with the landscape of Japan filled with broadleaved trees."

In the spring of 1873, Prime Minister Lee Yu-Won stated that "Cutting down trees with an ax has become worse until at last there is no tree at all in mountains. And the only reason is that the laws and ordinances have become loose." King Gojong responded, according to <*the Annals of Gojong*>, "Because pine trees used to grow so thickly in the surrounding mountains in the capital city, we were not able to see the ground before. However, they are so bare now that we can count how many pines there are."

Lieutenant Colonel Beverly also presented its causes. It was attributed to the unique heating structure of the Joseon houses that had smoke passages under the floor and furnaces outside that stirred up the unconscious and unproductive fuel consumption. He also considered that the intense cold temperature of the winter, the high density of the population, and the government's loose superintendence on cutting down trees were accelerating desolation of forest in the mountains.

Desolation of the Korean forest in the mountains has a long history. As the population grew at the beginning of the Joseon Dynasty, timber began to run short, because it was used almost exclusively as a building material for the palaces, Buddhist temples, military ships, gorgeous houses of high officials, and private houses. Under these circumstances, worries over the desolation of forest in the mountains started to appear on record from the middle of the Joseon Dynasty, and it had already reached a serious level by the end of the dynasty. Growth of population had destroyed the forests and mountains completely, starting around cities.

The Joseon Dynasty (1392-1910) formally put mountains and forests under the state's control and didn't allow ownership by private persons. But people could gather fuel wood from mountains without permission. That is, forest and mountains were perceived among the general population as land without owners, and they were neglected as such. Since all fuel wood was gathered from the mountains from the ancient period of the Three Kingdoms to the turn of the twentieth century, it was inevitable that the mountains would deteriorate. Also, the Ondol structure of houses under floor heating meant low energy efficiency and, therefore, a greater consumption of wood for fuel. In addition, more fuel wood was consumed as farmers in rural areas fed hot-boiled fodder to cows in the winter as a favor to them.

Naturally, illegal cutting to obtain timber or fuel wood was committed everywhere. In this regard, the Joseon Dynasty had a countermeasure called '*Geumsong*', which prohibited the cutting of pine trees. However, Geumsong and severe punishments were not enough to protect a forest in the mountains. Before many knew it, the mountains around the village became bald ones, and it became gradually impossible to hear a tiger's cry in Seoul. In 1910, growing stock volume (volume of standing trees per unit area) of Joseon (the entire Korean Peninsula) had been reduced to around 40m^3 per ha (hectare, 10,000m^2).

Photo 3. A picture that symbolically illustrates why and in what degree Joseon's mountains were bare. A bare mountain shown behind an inn in the Muak Pass in 1903, with an ox fully loaded with firewood on the back (a photo courtesy of ChosunIlbo)[30]

When the Joseon Dynasty population was twenty million people, and four hundred thousand people lived in Hanyang (presently Seoul), the capital city, all the mountains and fields outside of the Four Main Gates were the source of fuel wood for Hanyang. At this time, at a wood market right outside the southern Sigumoon Gate, horse carts and oxcarts carried firewood produced from the direction of Gwangju, while timbers coming from the direction of Yangju were sold right outside Dongsomun, and woods from Paju were sold outside West Main Gate. It was not difficult for Hanyang citizens to secure firewood if they had money at all. Construction timbers were transported from far-out Gangwon-do and Chungcheong-do on the Han River on floats. The rafts floating down on the Han River also transported the fuel from Yeoju, Icheon, and the Gwangju region halfway, which desolated mountain forests in these regions.

For more remote areas, fuel wood was actively bought and sold in accordance with market days at an interval of five days. Dry pine twigs and firewood from neighboring farm villages that were carried from early in the morning on A-frame carriers, oxen, or by women on their heads were sold in no time. In a word, firewood was a product that secured the easiest way to cash in. When forest rangers out from city and Gun (county) hall kept control, firewood was not allowed, but pine twigs were tolerated. Peasants had to pay a penalty if they got caught in action. On this occasion, peasants who were selling wood would say, "I cut down pine trees damaged by caterpillars." Or they said in deception, "I cut ones smoked and killed by a forest fire." after deftly burning the bark of firewood. [1]

Photo 4. To reach such a size, a tree must grow for over one hundred years. The Japanese cut and carried away such trees from the primeval forest.

Brutality of Japan

The essential misfortune of forest devastation didn't end there. As Japan won the Sino-Japanese War in 1895, it concluded the Treaty of Shimonoseki with China and secured the rights of cutting trees from around the Yalu (Aprok) River. It was ten years before the 1905 Convention was made up. Hindsight shows the depth of their ambition when they started securing cutting rights, taking advantage of the Joseon Dynasty's declining fortunes. Russia didn't idle away, either. In 1896 and 1903, it concluded the Korea-Russia Forest Convention with our country and secured the rights for cutting forests in the basin of the Aprok and the Duman River.

At that time, Japan and Russia had as massive forest resources as any country. In spite of that, they had marked out this small country for cutting out natural forests completely. On the other hand, what kind of men were the leaders of the Joseon Dynasty who were ready to hand over cutting rights? Japan, embezzling our country by the conclusion of the 1905 Convention, started to seize forest resources in full scale. At that time, mountain forests around villages had been decimated, but dense forests still stood in deep mountains hardly accessible to people.

Photo 5. Japanese imperialists felled at random and carried off by raft Korean white pines thickly grown in the neighborhood of the Aprok River and used them for constructing Manchuria.

As soon as Japan occupied Korea, it scrutinized all resources of Korea under the name of academic study. This included forest resources, and its survey was executed on the whole country. The Japanese established fourteen Regional Forest Offices around the country to manage and exploit the national forest, with eleven of them installed in Pyeongbuk, Hamnam, and Hambuk. From the Shinuiju, Hyesanjin, and Musan Regional Forest Offices, they cut out primeval forests on the shore of the Aprok River and the Duman River and around Baekdu Mountain, which had many dense forests. Before the 1905 Convention, Japan first cut down the primeval forest around Mt. Baekdu because of its victory in the Sino-Japanese War and carried the timber out using the Aprok and Duman Rivers. On the shores of the Aprok River, thick forest of Korean white pines had made a sea of trees. Japanese imperialists deforested this area in large quantities and, drawing the timber with rafts, used it for construction projects in the Manchurian region. In the same manner, Japanese militarists also exploited the thick forests in the southern part of the peninsula. Forestry statistics assembled for 1927 to 1941 remain to testify the brutality of Japanese imperialism. At this period, a total of 63 million m³ of growing stock volume decreased. Regionally, Hamnam recorded a decrease of 45.5 percent, Pyeongbuk 34.5 percent, and Hambuk 31.3 percent.

From the Bonghwa-Uljin region of Gyeongbuk, Japanese randomly cut off Geumgang pines measuring more than the length of one's arms in diameter, to which Ahn Se-Gi (age twenty, at the time of the Liberation) who lives at Guma Valley, Socheon-myeon, Bonghwa-gun, Gyeongbuk, testifies vividly. [1] At that time, the young Ahn got a job with the Joseon Forestry Development Corporation run by Japanese imperialists as a clerk for eight years, and there was a settlement of about ninety households of Japanese people working for this company in this neighborhood. The chief business of this company was to cut down the primeval forest, including Geumgang pines, all around Bonghwa-Uljin, usually employing two hundred to three hundred Joseon workers a day. Daily wages for one worker was 50 Jeon, so it was a moneymaking proposition that could buy two Mal (thirty-six liters) of rice by working five days. Trees cut down this way were dried at an open-air yard located at Hyeondong-myeon, Bonghwa-gun, until they were carried by train from Yeongju to Busan and then transported to Japan by ship. He said that the stump of a felled tree was large enough for four vigorous youths to have lunch on it. [1]

When, at the beginning of the 1940s, World War II reached its last stages, Japanese imperialists' plundering of forests ran to an extreme. They cut down trees of all the pine forests near villages and dug up all the stumps remaining to gather pine resin for use as military oil substitute, and they would not allow a single stump to remain by mobilizing the farming population of the entire country. This action aggravated landslides and floods in the rainy season, with mountain soil sweeping downward to rice paddies, dry fields, and rivers. It was because of this that in 1947, right after the Liberation, the extremely devastated regions of South Korea were in urgent need of erosion control projects for an area of 440,000 ha, and growing stock volume was only 8.8m³/ha.

Photo 6. For erosion control work, human sea tactics relying on a shovel and pick are the only answer. Picture shows erosion control work at Namsang-myeon, Geochang-gun, Gyeongnam Province in the middle of the 1930s. (photo courtesy of Yook Dong-Baek)

However, misfortunes didn't end yet. The Korean War (1950-1953), which occurred five years after the Liberation, made even the few trees remaining on this land the primary victims of its devastation. More horrible things were the social turmoil and poverty that ensued. Disorderly gathering of forest fuel and reckless deforestation in the state of administrative confusion during the Korean War and after was worth recording as a national shame. However, the destruction of forests at that time was a kind of indiscriminate felling for surviving economic difficulties, so any control without an alternative would have had a limited effectiveness. That was why the latter part of the 1950s was recorded in our history as the time of the worst dilapidation of forests. In 1956, the total area in desperate need of erosion control had increased to 686,000 ha, which meant that over ten percent of the forest area in South Korea was extremely devastated, resembling a desert. In addition, over half of the mountains were without trees. As the forests became more devastated, many serious side effects ensued. With even a little rain, earth was washed down from the mountains, raising the river beds and breaking embankments to bring about floods, which caused paddies and dry fields to be submerged. On the other hand, with a little drought, rivers dried out quickly, causing bad harvest almost every year. Fish disappeared from rivers, and birds and animals lost their habitats in the mountains. A rapid desertification of the country was destroying all ecosystems.

Chapter 2. Common Points of All Good Countries to Live in

Trees Are a National Wealth.

The Middle East is the birthplace of human civilization. However, losing the glories of the ancient times, it is now a widespread desert. While traveling the Middle East some time ago, the author experienced a sand desert that spread boundlessly, forbidding a single tree to grow and producing a suffocating heat. On my return home, Korea, seen from the sky, was thickened with trees everywhere, which set the author's mind at ease. Just a half century ago, however, Korea was covered with bald mountains like a semi-desert, no different from the Middle East, a fact hardly realized by younger generations of Koreans. The current old generations planted trees assiduously, sweating blood even in their extreme poverty, and recovered the old, beautiful land of Korea by preparing a site for their descendants' rich lives.

"Our ground doesn't give oil and gas like the Middle East does, but I really feel how large a blessing it is to be able to get water by digging any ground in the country. Oil and gas are the resources that will be gone as time passes, but water is the one that will eternally go on. Man doesn't suffer a great difficulty living without oil but cannot subsist even for a few days without water. I haven't realized it is a real blessing that we can easily get water of such immense price from anywhere." said Reverend Kim Jin-Hong at Durae Church (Oct 5, 2009).

They usually say, "Trees are a symbol of wealth," but the author thinks this is not an accurate expression. Trees are not a "symbol" of wealth, but are a "national wealth." Trees are a national wealth themselves next to industrial facilities or any kind of infrastructure of a country. The author's argument can be verified soon by looking at several of the most prosperous countries on this earth.

Common Points of the Four Major Advanced Countries

Germany is a country that built the foundation of modern forestry in the nineteenth century. This country is the origin of forestry (forest science), which is currently taught by each university of the world. Germany's dense forest supports this fact. Engaging in the First and Second World Wars, Germany became a defeated nation and had a very hard time economically. However, in the German people, there was a DNA to love and protect trees passing down through the generations. It was due to the education on the necessity and benefits of trees they received from elementary school days. That's why German people were not tempted to cut down and use an amount over a quota of trees during and even after the war. They had an underlying idea that they should not cut down and sell trees to fill their empty stomachs, even if they go hungry.

But the British army that occupied Germany couldn't believe its eyes. Dense forests, unlike what they saw at home, were covering the whole country. Especially in wartime, trees have an all-around use. The British army cut and used trees in the land of Germany as they pleased because it was the privilege of a victorious nation at war. However, the German people, even as a defeated nation, didn't accept this. They presented their petitions to the international organizations containing their vexation and mortification. The Queen of England, hearing the news that the German people were boiling over with rage, immediately ordered a stop to such behavior. Even now, the German people harvest timbers by the textbook, just as much as trees have grown. They take good care in planting and raising trees, with big pride of having dense forests. And they firmly keep their position as an economic powerhouse, ranking second or third in the world.

A long time ago, the United Kingdom (UK) was an island all covered with forests. In the beginning of the Industrial Revolution, however, they built iron-making industry by felling trees, and on the empty lots, they erected stock farms and kept sheep to activate the textile industry. As the Industrial Revolution continued, the UK's forest area decreased to around four percent of the country land. Then, a crisis came. After involvement in the two world wars, the country came to suffer a serious shortage of timber. It was no use crying over spilt milk.

Photo 7. The United States is the country that produces and consumes timber in the largest amount in the world but it also conserves its beautiful forests well.

After the end of World War II, the British government set about a nationwide reforestation project. The effect was doubled as it combined with creating jobs for soldiers who returned after the war. They built new houses, schools, and hospitals in mountain districts, and provided these people with villages to settle down. They organized professional tree-planting teams through training, and enforced a large-scale reforestation project, which resulted in a global model for reforestation. The UK is a country that once had a great territory over the world when it conquered the sea as a shipbuilding powerhouse. At that time, the whole of England was covered with forests that provided immense timbers. Again, the country is able to hold the position among the five strong countries of the world. This corresponds with the time when it has increased its forest area to over twelve percent of the country.

The United States is possessed of diverse forms of forests, from tropical to frigid ones worthy of the massive area of the country and is well-known for keeping its God-given natural beauty. Europe has had its forests mostly destroyed throughout its history of over a thousand years, with increased population and wars. However, the United States, in its short history of cultivation, has not repeated the mistakes Europe has made. Though in the 1850s, at the beginning of its frontier age, its citizens cut down the primeval forest in the Western region on a large scale, the country soon introduced the national parks system in 1872 for the first time in the world. Since then, the United States has been preserving the primeval forest in the Western region with a strong Nature Protection Act. When the Great Depression came at the beginning of the twentieth century, the federal government itself led a large-scale reforestation project to create employment.

Currently, the United States both produces and consumes largest amount of timber in the world. The country makes many of investments in education and research on forestry, leading forestry of the world in the twenty-first century in place of Germany. These days, chiefly large lumber companies own massive amounts of private land, leading to large-scale reforestation. That is, they plant southern pines that grow quickly on open fields deserted after farming in the southeastern region. They plant trees to harvest pulp in the southeastern region and trees to produce construction materials around the eastern Appalachian Mountains and western Rocky Mountains. Following public opinion and environmental groups, it is forbidden to harvest timber from national forests. From old times, campaigns for preserving trees and forests have been actively conducted, and the state of Nebraska designated Arbor Day for the first time in 1872.

Japan is a country with a warm and humid climate favorable to the growth of trees. Since it has had a long history of its own on the use of forest and trees, the Japanese preserve mountains and forests in a different way from other countries. Although they also had a history of forest destruction in some regions because of population increase and development of domestic industries at the beginning of the twentieth century, they consistently maintained excellent forests compared with the bare Korean Peninsula during the Joseon Dynasty period.

It is said that the Japanese came to Korea and disregarded Koreans during the occupation because Koreans had little regard for their own resources, cutting down trees in the mountains at random. Right after its defeat in World War II, Japan had a very hard time economically.

However, with all the people standing together, the Japanese have protected their forests. In the hearts of people who wanted the country to advance, there was also a beautiful disposition to love nation's trees and forest. Ultimately, Japan was able to develop into a great economic power against all odds.

Japan maintains its beautiful man-made forests by developing tree species that are easy to propagate and that have a high value as timber, such as Sugi and Hinoki. The Japanese plant these trees on a large scale as part of Japan's active reforestation project. Although the country imports the most tropical timbers in the world and is sometimes criticized for abetting in the destruction of tropical forests, it also produce a very large domestic timber crop. Because people insist on wooden houses as a guard against Japan's frequent earthquakes, the nation has a tradition of managing trees and forests wisely over time and of recognizing the true value of forests.

These are not mere coincidences. It is absolutely true that the world's most prosperous countries have good forests. So do they have good forests because they are well-off? Or are they well-off because they have good forests? We do not have to argue which is first. However, it is obvious that being well-off and having good forests are linked and mutually necessary.

Photo 8. Japanese Sugi in Japan looks like a twin in the growing pace and shape due to propagation by cutting, which makes a unique beautiful forest.

There are still other interesting testimonies. Let me introduce just two of them. When Park Chung-Hee went to the United States for study as an artillery officer, he saw the affluence of green forests. And when he later visited Germany as president of Korea, he learned that trees were not just a part of nature, but a symbol of wealth itself. During these first-hand encounters with foreign countries and in conversations with many people, he learned that a common characteristic of prosperous countries was their dense forests, preserved by taking good care of nature. [2]

President Park's dream was to restore the greenery in the mountain hills in his homeland. He drove strongly reforestation projects during the eighteen years of his reign, and was successful in stopping further expansion of denuded lands. A report by FAO in 2005 indicates that the earth's total forest area continues to decrease at about 13 million hectares per year, twice the size of total forest land area of South Korea. Over the past fifty years, 650,000 km^2 of land in the world has become desert. That is over six times the size of South Korea. According to UN statistics, the desert area was annually increasing 1,600 km^2 in the 1970s, 2,100 km^2 in the 1980s and 3,560 km^2 in the 1990s, reaching a total of 12 million km^2 of deserts on the global basis. These numbers show that desertification is going on faster recently. Expansion of desert includes an advanced country like the United States as well as developing countries in Africa, Asia, and South America, but Korea is an exception. It is a great fortune. Although our people had lived worrying about flood, drought, and food shortages, even up until recently, it seems Korea finally has the necessary and sufficient conditions to join the ranks of good countries to live in.

Chapter 3. The First Republic after the 1945 Liberation

Korea's First Celebration of Arbor Day

After the 1945 Liberation of Korea, the US military administration established April 5 as Arbor Day, recognizing the importance of planting trees. It came from the tradition that it was April 5 when King Seongjong in the Joseon Dynasty, leading his prince and civil and military officials, held a ceremony for a good harvest at Seonnongdan (a farming promotion platform) located just outside East Gate, plowing the ground himself.

After establishing the Arbor Day, detailed records remain for the fourth Arbor Day celebration dated April 5, 1949.[1] President Rhee Syng-Man, Kim Gu, and Kim Gyu-Shik, participated at the ceremony held at Hannam Elementary School. It seems that, at that time, Arbor Day events had political meanings. That was why, despite the dreary weather of sleeting from the early morning, hundreds of people, including figures holding important positions in the government, Seoul citizens, forest officials, among others, headed for the event. Important figures made speeches that day.

President Rhee Syng-Man said in his speech, "Our thirty million countrymen should stand together in making the desolated mountains and forests green and taking good care of them to recover our ancient picture of scenic beauty as soon as possible, for which I propose to everyone here making a pledge by holding up our hands."

Kim Gu said, "This land of ours is literally a country noted for picturesque rivers and mountains. With good mountains and good waters, it used to be a good place to live. But the Japanese militarists invaded this country with ambition and military force, plundered rice we farmed by the sweat of our brow, felled the dense primeval forests in Mt. Baekdu at random, transported them in rafts by the Aprok River, lumbered this by installing a sawmill in Shinuiju and took them as military materials in order for Gwandong Army in Manchuria to invade China. Now that Japan has been defeated, we fellow countrymen should all keep on caring for the mountains together with heart."

Dr. Kim Gyu-Shik said, "Because of the muddy water of China's Yellow River, the West Sea has now come to be called the Yellow Sea. The Chinese say that the ruler of the Yellow River ought to be a national leader. Leaders should direct much energy and all the nation should cooperate for our country's conservation of rivers and forests. We should not make a fuss only on Arbor Day but make steady and persistent efforts with a long view."

Photo 9. Although Rhee Syng-Man, the first president, attended the Arbor Day event annually, his forest policy failed to bear much fruit.

But no one mentioned that "The government is going to do this, so all our nation is asked to help the government by doing that." Regrettably, the politicians stressed only what the people should do. This omission meant the government practically had no blue-print prepared, so we can see that this Arbor Day celebration was no more than a political event.

President Rhee Syng-Man's Struggle

As an administrator, Korea's first president Rhee Syng-Man seems to have taken much interest in forestry or forest reclamation. However, he wasn't lucky. He devised and enforced a number of new reforestation projects with extremely meager results. First, he drove forward the Ten-Year Reforestation and Erosion-Control Plan (1948-1957). Due to the lack of finances and the Korean War, however, he performed only erosion control work on a total of 44,000 ha for ten years and the actual numbers were not confirmed later (Office of Forestry, <*100 Years of Korea's Erosion Control*>)[3]. In addition, in the days of the Busan Refuge Government, he enacted the Temporary Forest Protection Act in 1951. It was an urgent measure made in anarchy during the War; because the secret felling of trees was rampant, and deforestation accelerated. The Act attempted to take strides in emergency erosion control and to reforest barren land with fast-growing trees such as the black locust, alder, and pitch pine among others. However, the plan failed to be executed properly because the government was confronted with a double and triple whammy of a lack of financial resources, techniques, and enthusiasm.

His administration also set up the Three-Year Reforestation Plan (1952-1954), the Five-Year Erosion Control Plan (1953-1957), and the Second Ten-Year Private Forest Reforestation Plan (1954-1963). These were initiated by the UNKRA (UN Korean Reconstruction Agency) aid project during the Korean War to seek a plan for securing fuel wood for heating Ondol rooms when the timber supply got short. At that time, wheat flour was distributed to workers instead of wages, so it was also nicknamed as the "wheat flour erosion control." This project may have contributed to the start of creating fuel-wood forests after the launch of the Korean government, but there was no big result harvested. Records indicate the deforestation area as of 1956 was 686,230 ha [3].

A new reforestation project was also started by the aid of the United States. The ICA (International Cooperation Agency) supported Korea's postwar rehabilitation project after the Korean War and reestablished the Five-Year Erosion Control plan (1957-1961) and established the Ten-Year Upstream Soil and Water Conservation Plan (1958-1967). The latter was a project for sowing hay seed introduced from the United States on the upstream catchment area in order to prevent the efflux of soil from the mountains.

Photo 10. Despite the shortage of domestic sources of timber in the 1950s, timber for railroad ties collected from a national forest at Mt. Hambaek, Jungseon-gun, Gangwon-do, had a considerably large diameter.

From the Japanese Occupation, erosion control work in Korea employed a strip sodding method of construction, which was composed of terracing on a slope, building up stone walls, adding fertile soil brought from outside, and then sodding. However, the ICA advisory group insisted on the American method of sowing American hay seed which was composed of orchard grass, weeping love grass, switch grass, Kentucky blue grass, and fescue, among others. These are the grasses chiefly used for making a golf course green these days. In the first year, addition of fertilizer components caused good germination, but then new shoots died of drought and lack of nutrients the following year. As it turned out, the hay seed improved in the United States failed to adapt to the climate of Korea. Around 100 tons of seeds were sown in accordance with this project, but the project was interrupted soon with poor results.

The United States enacted Public Law (PL) 480 to supply food to the extremely poor, backward countries of the world. Accordingly, after the Korean War, the United States contributed grains for tree-planting projects to rehabilitate the devastated region through the ICA. To farming people mobilized for the reforestation project, grains were provided in place of wages, and these ICA-supported grains played decisive role in mobilizing the idle labor of rural communities.

Even after the end of the Korean War, mountain forests in Korea continued to follow the path of dilapidation. Pine caterpillars, with a destructive power next to human illegal cutting and indiscriminate felling, were the culprits. Right after the Liberation, damage by caterpillars to pine forests was on the slow increase. As mountain forests became suffered from the devastation of the Korean War, however, damage by caterpillars increased rapidly in the latter part of the 1950s.

From 1957 to 1961, frequent floods caused large casualties and property damage. Flood damage in the five years amounted to 1,300 casualties, 199,000 ha of farmland lost or buried, and 220,000 victims. The records show a close correlation between dilapidated mountain forests and disasters, as the area of extremely dilapidated mountain forests increased to 680,000 ha in the latter part of the 1950s.

Photo 11. President Yun Bo-Seon (leftmost in the picture) directed the planting of trees in relation to construction of the country but couldn't contribute significantly to forest reclamation because of his short period in office. The picture shows apathetic bare mountain behind (March 1, 1961).

In 1959, at the close of President Rhee's seizure of power, his government set up a "Five-Year Plan for Fuel-Wood Forest Establishment" and held an event titled "National Rally for Promotion of the Erosion Control Project" at Sadang-ri, Shiheung-gun, Gyeonggi-do, showing an amazing will of the government by the participation of thousands of people, including the president and the American ambassador. At that time, our country had 2.4 million farmhouses, and the plan was to plant fuel-wood forests on an area of 0.5 ha per house in order to have an annual five tons of fuel supplied to each household. In addition to the 400,000 ha already made, it was planned to reforest a new 800,000 ha, but the military coup broke out in 1961, and the project didn't go off properly. To sum up, the Rhee Syng-Man government took an interest in reforestation, put forward many projects, and even received support from the United States, but most resulted in failure due to impractical plans, and a lack of ambition.

Photo 12. The A-frame was an extremely convenient means of transport for moving seedlings or fertilizer to a high mountain. It was also misused for forest destruction by carrying timber, fuel wood, and leaf litter.

One tragic state of things would be enough to finish the actual condition of reforestation under the Rhee Syng-Man government. It was in 1960, the year when April 19 Revolution occurred. Kim Gap-Seong, of the Bureau of Forestry, Ministry of Agriculture and Forestry, was assigned to Mt. Jiri in Hamyang, Gyeongnam, as head of the Regional Forest Office. With a management area of around 20,000 ha, it had a staff of two persons without any means of transportation. At that time, the situation was so dire that while illegal cutters ran away with trees carried in a GMC truck, a forest ranger had to chase after them barefooted. It is said that Kim Gap-Seong begged the Agricultural Experiment Station, a higher institution, for transportation, and barely was able to have one jeep allocated to it. This story indicates that, at that time, those beautiful trees in Mt. Jiri had been completely exposed to forest tree thieves.

More shocking is the story told by Kim Sa-Il, who was newly assigned to the same place in December, 1961.[1] There were illegal charcoal kilns in every valley. They were spouting out flames glaringly. He seized one to three thousand charcoal sacks a day, and saws and axes taken from tree thieves were piled up high. More shocking was the fact that charcoal sacks piled up by seizure were sometimes stolen in a single night, he says. Without the collusion and cooperation of the police, it would have been impossible to carry out stolen trees because there was a lift arm gate in front of the police box or a branch office at the entrance of the mountain, but this was what happened anyway.

Reforestation under the thirteen years (1948 to 1960) of the Rhee Syng-Man administration can be summarized in figures like this: a total of 2.8 billion trees were planted in a total area of 1.05 million ha, while the growing stock volume of the 1950s forests was 5.6m³/ha, with 50 percent bare mountains (treeless ground), and an area in desperate need of erosion control of 680,000 ha. In 1961 the growing stock volume of forests across the country was only 11 m³/ha. Compared with official growing stock volume of 126 m³/ha for 2011, this figure showed that the mountains were extremely desolated, and the volume of standing trees in the mountains at that time was only 8.7 percent of that in 2011.

Part 2.

Park Chung-Hee's Comet-like Appearance

Chapter 4. General Park, Leader of the Military Revolution

May-16 Military Coup

On May 16, 1961, a military coup d'état broke out. One year earlier, student uprisings on April 19 occurred because it was a time when chaos, disorder, and poverty were rampant politically and socially. However, this event only initiated motivation, revealing its limitations in disposing of the social turmoil, and contributed to setting the stage for the military with a strong leadership coming forward.

But why should Park Chung-Hee come to power? He had serious flaws within the military organization in relation to his past career as a pro-communist as well as a military career as a member of the Japanese army. How was it possible for one who had such shortcomings to become general, find credence with the military leadership, and finally be selected and supported as the revolution leader by high-ranking officers?

There may be many reasons for this, but from the author's viewpoint, it can be boiled down to his leadership and integrity. First, as to leadership, he had a logical mind and the ability to make plans. He was aboveboard in everything and a man of great insight as well. Second, he was a man of integrity without selfishness. In his usual action and behavior, he put the nation before his interests and ambitions, keeping to his definite cause all the time. This feature of his personality was illustrated in the support demonstration by the military cadets right after the Coup. Even after rising to presidency, he made a constant effort toward national interests without laying an eye on his and his relatives' gains or fame, a fact that must have caused many people in posterity to describe his initiated action as a "revolution".

There is another mystery. In the suddenly increased social turmoil in the aftermath of the student uprising of April 19, 1960, there was a piecemeal leak of rumors from the military that Major General Park Chung-Hee had been ready for a coup. There even is a record that this kind of information was reported to then-President Yun Bo-Seon or Prime Minister Chang Myun. So what is it that prevented the president or the Chief of the General Staff from stopping this in advance? One interpretation suggested that it was because the military, especially its generals, who knew well about Major General Park's integrity and leadership, were implicitly in favor of his intended coup.

Photo 13. Right after the May 16 military coup, the military rounded up gangsters from around the country to be brought to the people's judgment. This was a starting point of social purification efforts cheered by the whole nation (May 21, 1961).

In this regard, here's a recollection by Professor Kim Byeong-Hee, Dean of Hanyang University Liberal Arts College (an alumnus from Park Chung-Hee's Daegu School of Education) [5].

When, after Park's request for help as a friend, I visited Park's office as the Supreme Council chairman right after his revolution, I found Park's office as miserable as a battlefield commander's. His chair was like a wooden chair placed before a shoeshine boy by the wayside. In addition, he was smoking "Arirang", a domestic brand of tobacco, while I enjoyed the highest-class "Cheongja", not to mention Western tobaccos I was frequently presented with. The next time when I called on him again, Park Chung-Hee was having his lunch by 10-won's-worth (US 15 cents) of noodles in soup served hot in a casserole dish garnished with several pieces of Dakuan (Japanese style kimchi). Since on that day I had eaten my lunch for 500 won (US $7.50) with my friends, the sight went home to my heart.

Another testimony by Lee Sang-Hun, 11th Korean Military Academy (later, Minister of National Defense), confirms Park's frugality.[5] When Chairman Park stayed at a hotel after attending a pro-revolution rally held in Gwangju, Lee saw Park washing and hanging his socks on the line in the restroom late at night. Chairman Park himself looked self-conscious. He was so thrifty that he did not have enough socks with him.

Samuel D. Berger, the American ambassador to Korea, reported the following message by telegraph to his State Department on October 28, 1961, which well showed the unselfish picture of the revolutionary government. [5]

"It has been five months since the military regime stepped in. Despite some bad foreign impression from its authoritative and military nature, this administration is passionate, sincere, and filled with vision and willpower. Although failing to win positive support from the general public, they, starting with up-down revolution in a true sense of the word, are driving forward a sweeping essential reform. Reform projects, which were only discussed or conceived in the previous government, such as bank credit policies, international trade, expansion of public works for the unemployed, countermeasures for tax evasion, measures for farming and labor union, sectors of education and administration, welfare (reform of prisons, rehabilitation of prostitutes, family plan projects, support of wounded soldiers and policemen and bereaved children), are now being effectively carried out. Many of these reforms are positive and the result of taking advice from the United States...... The military government's crackdown on cornering and hoarding, bribery, close relationships between political and business circles, smuggling, illegal cutting, embezzlement of military supplies, gangsters, and blackmail by the police and reporters is already working. Investigations of communists' penetration maneuvers and the anti-communist propaganda have increased both in quality and quantity."[5]

Photo 14. A sight in the vicinity of Munsan Station, Gyeonggi-do at the beginning of the 1960s. It reminds us of the American West. At that time, this kind of bare landscape was seen anywhere in Korea.

On November 16, 1961, after meeting American President John F. Kennedy, Chairman Park Chung-Hee delivered an address at the National Press Club in Washington, which includes the following as part.

"Under the circumstances of the corruption of society, bureaucracy, labor groups' intervention in politics, buying of the press, the mass being infected with communism, and, in all this confusion, even usurious private lenders taking sides with oppression, I carried out the revolution by mustering about 220 integral and devoted colleagues which was expanded from a dozen of the key force in the revolution. After the revolution,......... we set about the urgent waterway construction, the reforestation project and the reclamation work and provided jobs for tens of thousands of people."[5]

In his speech overseas before the local press he even mentioned the reforestation project, which might have seemed trivial, which shows that he had significant interest in this area.

Scraping out of the Five Major Social Ills: Illegal Cutting

On May 20, 1961, four days after the coup, General Jang Gyeong-Sun, in his military uniform, burst into the office of the Minister of Agriculture and Forestry under the escort of five mid-level officers wearing pistols[1]. It was the government office building for the Ministry of Agriculture and Forestry located in Seodaemun-gu at that time. General Jang, who was inaugurated as the new Minister of Agriculture and Forestry, immediately had a briefing from Lee Won-Han, reforestation section chief, on many reforestation projects in effect. Then, by calling out Shim Jong-Seop, the Forest Bureau head, he ordered that 0.5 ha fuel-wood forest per household in rural community should be planted immediately. It was an order to be enforced even by requisitioning private lands. Although later the clause of requisition was deleted, the military government knew from the beginning that for forest reclamation, it was of the most urgent necessity to solve the problem of lack of fuel for farm villages. This action provided a sure impetus for the fuel-wood forest establishment project, which had been progressing at a snail's pace. [1]

Another thing to remember as one of the military government's achievements is its quick measure of controlling pine caterpillars. At that time, damage from pine caterpillars was extremely heavy across the country. So Professor Shin Jae-Sang, of the Department of Forestry at Seoul National University, searched the forests around the country for microorganisms acting as a caterpillar's natural enemy. After years of research, he found in 1957 white muscardine fungus (*Beauveria bassiana)*, which hardens and kills the body of caterpillars, and made a plan to multiply and spread it in forests to reduce damage from caterpillars. Put in today's term, it was a pioneering introduction of an eco-friendly extermination of pests using its natural enemy. Right on time, the military government took the lead by commanding a mass dispersal of the fungus. It was a rare case of government-academy cooperation.

Damage from caterpillars has greatly decreased since the latter part of the 1970s. Thick forests increased soil moisture, killing most of larvae hibernating in the moistened soil and reducing damage spontaneously. Nowadays, damage is found only on some islands in the south. In the case of North Korea, report has it that the pine forests have been getting more and more desolated until today there is serious damage because the soil has become dry enough to suit the successful hibernation of caterpillars.

Photo 15. Black locust, which not only enriched the barren soil within a short period but also served as a fuel-wood forest, finished its duties, which continued for half a century, with no more use in the twenty-first century.

In its revolution pledge, the military government laid down the Five Major Social Ills as smuggling, drugs, illegal cutting, gangsters, and quasi-reporters. The inclusion of illegal cutting here showed that Park Chung-Hee had a particular interest in the matter of deforestation from the start of his revolution. Accordingly, in June 1961, the next month after the revolution, the military government enacted the "Forest Products Regulation Act." This law created a very strong policy of protecting forests, including forest products regulation, enforcement of compulsory reforestation by institutions, coupled with the beefed-up action of restricting entrance to forests.

This law interrupted all domestic production and carrying out of forest products and systemized "a forest product carrying-out certificate" issued by mayors and Gun (county) heads to be checked at each railroad station, which was subject to another regulation at Seoul Station for the sake of a thorough implementation of the law. Additionally, in case a vehicle carrying an illegal forest product was caught, it was subjected to cancellation of the vehicle's registration.

The tense and violent atmosphere right after the coup worked in a practical manner on the crackdown. However, cunning illegal cutters continued their trade by felling trees exceeding their limits, by forging seals on the trees cut down, by dealing in black-market carrying-out certificates and manipulating them by hiding timbers without seals deep inside of their trucks, as well as by colluding with inspecting policemen, all of which posed difficulties in promptly eradicating illegal cutting. On the other hand, the action taken at the beginning of the revolution of fully stopping forest products was cancelled in three months due to strong protests from the mining industry, which argued that this action would also cause failure in producing mine timbers and then in production of coal. Later it was found that increased production of coal was another main project that Chairman Park had put emphasis on.

Enactment of the First Forest Law

On December 27, 1961, seven months after taking power, the military government enacted the Forest Law (Act No. 881) at last. Enactment of this law has a very important meaning since it was the first act in the history of our country in relation to the forests and forestry. Although, after the Liberation, the Rhee Syng-Man government knew well the importance of forest protection, it failed to enact the forest law and remained at promulgating the Temporary Forest Protection Act in 1951 to prevent the damage to forests caused by the Korean War. And the Forest Products Regulation Act hurriedly enacted right after the 1961 revolution was just a temporary and partial act.

The 1961 Forest Law was the fourth act enacted and promulgated by the military government except for temporary acts, which reflects the fact that its leader was well aware of the importance of forest protection. The laws made by the military government before this forest law were just three; the Anti-Communist Law (July 3, 1961), the Export Association Law, and the Industrial Standards Act. The figure in power will enact the most needed law first, and what is most urgent depends on his ruling philosophy.

Photo 16. Italian poplars, well-known for being fast growing like bamboo shoots, were planted along the river banks in the 1960s with the desperate need for early reforestation, and served the use of timber for boards and boxes, and the reforestation of our country.

The forest law made at this opportunity stipulated and governed all matters over the forests, and was intended to act as the mother law in-so-far as mountain forests were concerned. It was made with a design to sustain the development of the national economy by protecting and cultivating the forest, increasing forest resources, and conserving national land. Especially, the law stipulated forming a Forestry Cooperative for each village to make fuel-wood forests, which contributed largely to developing a sense of cooperation, a basic spirit for the Saemaul Movement that was to occur later.

The Forest Law covers the following:

1. Erosion-control project for restoring desolated lands, fuel-wood forest establishment, and plans for detailed forest protection

2. Expanded supply of smokeless coal and plans for saving consumption of forest fuel: Banning carry-in of forest fuel and expanding supply of smokeless coal for Seoul and Gyeonggi-Inchon area with large populations

3. Improvement of farm village furnaces to burn the least amount of wood

4. Plans for securing firewood: Establish obligatory fuel-wood forest by residents' cooperation so that gathering fuel wood may be banned altogether from other places than fuel-wood forests.

5. Form a forestry cooperative in each village to make residents participate in the forest projects (e.g., establishing fuel-wood forest)

On January 15, 1962, the next year of the revolution, the government enacted and promulgated the "Erosion Control Act" and set about concrete enforcement for large-scale erosion control planting. Its first step was a mass production of planting stocks. With a view to secure a number of planting stocks in a short period, the government attempted to raise planting stocks using existing village forestry cooperatives. In return for posting 460 nursery specialists in the whole country and paying them an exceptional level of remuneration, the government demanded each one of them to successfully produce 1 to 1.5 million seedlings of black locust annually through their village forestry cooperative. It was a plan to produce methodically over 500 million black locust seedlings annually within a short period.

At that time, as the farm village scraped out even the last bits of fallen leaves under the difficulty of meeting fuel-wood requirements, the earth, after losing all mineral nutrients, was turning into bare mountains rapidly. The soil of the mountain forests had become so dry and barren that a normal tree couldn't grow up. However, black locust, a leguminous plant with root nodules, makes the soil fertile by transforming nitrogen gas in the air into an organic nitrogenous compound. It seems that the military government was persuaded that planting black locust en masse was the only way, after listening to the experts' opinions. The black locusts planted then in tremendous numbers served to improve the soil of the mountains and forests of the whole country steadily for forty years thereafter. Black locust has a short lifespan of forty to fifty years. After that, black locusts died gradually, while in more fertile soil, oaks and other broadleaved trees have grown up until making a beautiful and dense forest we can see these days.

In these processes of a large-scale reforestation, there is one thing we cannot overlook. It was a revival of the Village Forestry Cooperative, which actively participated in the erosion control works. The Village Forestry Cooperative was a successor of the Village Pine Cooperative, which had been handed down from the Joseon Dynasty, ordered to break up in 1932 under the Japanese occupation, and reconstructed after the Liberation. At the end of 1952, the Village Forestry Cooperative around the country had 21,570 local chapters, with a membership of two million households, but there was a slump in activity except when their members were mobilized for the project of exterminating pine caterpillars.

After the enactment of the Forest Law in 1962, a short-term intensive erosion-control planting project (1963-1964) was established in order to complete reforestation for 380,000 ha of bare mountains for two years. In this regard, the government was planning to bear the expenses only for materials and the groundwork, while securing labor by mobilizing local Village Forestry Cooperative members. To legalize the needed compulsory labor, the government promulgated the Temporary Act of Forest Reclamation in February of 1963.

According to the reforestation schedule, gathering seeds was carried out across the country by mobilizing Village Forestry Cooperative members, resulting in a total of 1,035,000 kg of seeds, including black locust (142,000 kg), *Lespedeza* (378,000 kg), common grasses (461,000 kg), and legume plants (54,000 kg). In this erosion-control planting, 2.4 million man-days of Village Forestry Cooperative members were mobilized from 1963 to 1964 to complete reforestation for 374,000 ha. At last, based on this spirit of cooperation and success, the Village Forestry Cooperative organization took the lead in the Saemaul reforestation project as Saemaul Movement started in 1971.

Poplar Planting National Movement

In 1962, the next year of the revolution, the Poplar Planting National Movement was spread. *Hankook Ilbo* daily news and the Korea Poplar Commission in partnership spread the movement of planting poplars on riversides and vacant lots around the country. In particular, the Poplar Commission recommended Italian poplars improved by Dr. Hyun Shin-Kyu at Seoul National University. At that time, *Hankook Ilbo* was making a large poplar plantation on the river bank of the South Han River, and its president Jang Gi-Yeong was actively engaged in supplying poplars by buying the cuttings at his own expense and sending them to the provinces. This newspaper also started a fund-raising campaign, and President Park sent his contribution on February 1, 1965, complimenting that "This campaign will not only facilitate the reforestation project driven in an effort for the Five-Year Economic Development Plan but will also make a shortcut to reconstruct the poor farm villages."

The Poplar Planting Movement became more active after Jang Gi-Yeong was appointed as Deputy Prime Minister of Finance and Economy. In the afternoon of March 6 (Sunday), 1966, he ushered President Park in person to the poplar plantation on the South Han River. President Park looked very pleased, embracing, shaking, and even hanging on the trees. "It's a great success. There are many waste-lands in this country, so we should spread such a fast-growing tree quickly and make a profitable reforestation."[2]

I, the author, was senior in high school in 1962 and came to learn from reports in the papers and radio that fast-growing poplars would contribute greatly to reforestation of the denuded country. This changed my mind into majoring in forestry, which drew little interest from people then, although I had set my heart on an engineering career. Despite great opposition from my parents and family members, I finally entered the Department of Forestry at Seoul National University and learned from Professor Hyun Shin-Kyu. I feel a great reward in my life from having specialized in forestry especially in work related to the reforestation of my country for about fifty years so far.

From 1963, the Forestry Cooperative Federation encouraged the planting of a hundred Italian poplar trees for each farmhouse around the house, river bank, and cultivated land. Through 1970, a total of twenty million poplar trees were planted nationwide. Thereafter, the poplar planting movement became an opportunity to introduce the idea of a collective farm in the farm village. Profits made from jointly raising and selling the poplar cuttings were converted into a fund to be used for scholarships for students entering high school, which earned the name of "poplar scholarships". In 1967, President Park sent 14,000 poplar trees to Cheongwon-gun, Chungbuk, which planted them on the Miho stream bank and launched a poplar scholarship foundation.[2] Because of the poplar scholarships, every village eagerly planted poplars, which resulted in a total planting area of 730,000 ha across the country until

1985. It was a whopping number.

As time passed, however, there occurred a civil appeal that poplars planted on riversides interrupted the flow of river water during annual flooding in a rainy season, which contributed to inundation. The appeal brought about changing the River and Stream Law, and no further planting of poplars has been allowed.

Photo 17. The black locust has many uses in bare, desolate mountains. It enriches the soil, grows fast to provide fuel wood, produces good quality honey, and even reduces soil erosion by keeping the surface soil from being washed off. The picture shows the success of reclamation in four years after planting black locusts.

On December 3, 1962, recognizing the importance of our culture, the military government enacted the "Cultural Treasure Protection Law" for the first time. Based on this law, the government designated and protected palaces, Buddhist temples, beauty spots, historical sites, old trees in villages, historical trees, tree native habitats, and groves as natural monuments to contribute to the protection of trees and forests. Also, in July 1961, right after the military revolution, the revolutionary government ordered first the restoration of National Treasure Number One, Sungryemun (known as South Gate) in Seoul, which had been broken in the Korean War, and had it completed in May 1963.

There is an incident still publicly unknown. On July 18, 1962, there was a bill for cutting financial aid to Korea submitted by the US Congress. It insisted that with the country's unstable political situation in 1960 and

1961 and lack of clear economic development so far, there was no need to continue aiding Korea for over a decade. At this time, Alexander Wiley, a senator from the State of Wisconsin, made a speech purporting that financial aid to Korea had not been in vain because the pitch-lolly pine developed by Dr. Hyun Shin-Kyu at Seoul National University was making the American forests green. Plans for cutting aid were vetoed. This fact was naturally conveyed to Chairman Park, who must have had his eye specifically on Dr. Hyun from that point.

A5500   CONGRESSIONAL RECORD — APPENDIX

What Foreign Countries Can Do for Us

EXTENSION OF REMARKS
OF
HON. ALEXANDER WILEY
OF WISCONSIN
IN THE SENATE OF THE UNITED STATES
Wednesday, July 18, 1962

Mr. WILEY. Mr. President, for a long time, the United States has been supporting programs for assistance to other nations.

The best kind of relationships between ourselves and such recipient countries, however, requires a two-way—not a one-way—street for interchange of ideas, goods, and other values.

WONDER PINE TREE FROM KOREA

A Korean forestry expert, Dr. Sin Kyu Hyun, has developed a remarkable new hybrid pine tree—from pitch and loblolly pines—at the Korean Institute of Forest Genetics in Suwan. It grows rapidly and produces an excellent quality of wood. Most important, it prospers in a cold climate, unlike most of our commercial southern loblolly pine.

The U.S. Forest Service is giving the new pine tree extensive field tests in Illinois. It may revolutionize our northern woods.

Photo 18. In July 1962, a bill was submitted to the US Senate to cut down aid to Korea. At this time, Senator Wiley emphasized that aid to Korea had not been in vain, pointing to the fact that a new variety of pine bred by Dr. Hyun Shin-Kyu was growing well in the northern part of the US. The bill for cutting aid was rejected after all.

In 1963, the next year, President Park appointed Dr. Hyun as the second Rural Development Administration head. Although Dr. Hyun was already a prominent figure in the circles of forestry as president of the Korea Forestry Society, it was a very rare case that a person majoring in forestry was appointed as the head of the Rural Development Administration. Maybe Senator Wiley's remark had some influence or it was a personnel shift that foreshadowed the all-out movement of reforestation to be evolved thereafter. Anyway, even after Dr. Hyun resigned from the post later, President Park tried to listen to the views of Dr. Hyun on reforestation and maintained a special relationship by presenting him a car and other gifts.

Chapter 5. Park Chung-Hee in His Younger Days

His Days at Daegu School of Education

What was the young Park Chung-Hee like before he became the leader of a country? From the standpoint of this book, he seems to have been rather effeminate in his early days. A few poems of his writing remain that don't particularly show a literary talent. It was also not certain whether he had the broad views or deep discrimination to quality as a ruler; because his school record reveals that he became the president of class simply for his good work at subjects. Notable is the fact that he was good at science courses like math as well as liberal arts courses like social studies or history. This knowledge leads one to surmise that he had his right and left side of the brain, that is, his emotion and reason, developed in equal proportion.

All in all, Park Chung-Hee, in his young days, seems to have been a petty bourgeois devoid of any opportunity to exercise his spirit of nationalism or patriotic sentiment while in search of his future path, but just an ordinary soldier without being thorough in the military spirit so as to be labeled as pro-communist at one time. Of course, he was generous in being considerate of his men and adhered to his principle of not feathering his nest.

Park Chung-Hee was born on the fourteenth of November, 1917 in a village at the foot of Mt. Geumo, called Moraesil, Sangmo-ri, Gumi-myeon, Seonsan-gun, Gyeongbuk. It was the place from which the Nakdong River was seen in the distance. He was the youngest of five sons and two daughters in a poor farm family. Though born at a farm village of extreme poverty, he was able to receive a healthy home training through the careful love of his mother and siblings. After he entered Gumi Elementary School at Gumi-eup in 1926, he attended school on foot, 16 km both ways, every day for six years. Probably it was not an easy distance for the little boy Park Chung-Hee, who was considerably smaller than others.

Photo 19. Park Chung-Hee was born in this shabby, stable-like house, located at Sangmo-dong, Gumi-myeon, Seonsan-gun, Gyeongbuk Province.

He was the best student from the third grade and was automatically selected as the monitor (class president now) until he graduated from the school. His leadership was remarkable, and he had the nickname of "jujube cudgel" (a stout-minded man) because there was a firm character about him. He had a great memory and excelled in math, geography, and history. In 1931, in his sixth grade, he read Lee Gwang-Su's novel <*Lee Sun-Shin*> (a general who saved the Joseon Dynasty from Japanese invasion in sixteenth century) that began appearing in *Dong A Ilbo* daily news serially. Reading the novel was possible because his third eldest brother, who was working at Gumi-eup, sent him the newspaper, and the story had a big effect on building the little boy's character. Not talkative, he didn't make many friends, but he was intelligent, cool-headed, and rather meditative.

The pine grove path on the way to school was so thick with trees that occasionally a wolf appeared and no one could pass it through alone. When he revisited his hometown after the Liberation, he found that it had turned into a bald hill with all the trees cut down. This sight broke the heart of the young Park Chung-Hee.

After graduating from Gumi Elementary School in 1932, he entered Daegu School of Education for the first time from his small home town, Sangmori. During his attendance, he even had a longtime absence because he failed to pay the monthly tuition fee. It is not well known what his idea was about the mountains and forests of his mother country in his high school days. There is only one thing that after his return from his observation tour to Mt. Geumgang (the most beautiful mountain in Korea and known as Diamond Mountain) in 1934, his third year in high school, one poem he wrote illustrates his love of the country and trees when he was still a youth.

Mt. Geumgang!

A noted mountain of the world with twelve thousand peaks
While you are most reputed for the scenic beauty and solemnity
We are so desolated in the same country
I am so ashamed to you I cannot hold my head before you
Mt. Geumgang!
We promise you to be just as brilliant and shining as you with struggle

Written by Chung-Hee at Onjeong-ri

Daegu School of Education Newsletter No. 4 (1936) published his poem and showed how Park Chung-Hee in his fifth year expressed the beauty of a wild-flower and the importance of farmers. There seems to be some connection to Park's initiative in the nature conservation movement and his leading role in rural community revival for farmers and the Saemaul Movement afterwards.

Mother Nature

1. More gracious and more beautiful
   Is the wild flower
   That has come out shyly on the corner of a wilderness
   Than a brilliant rose in the garden

2. Nobler and more beautiful
   Is the farmer who brings the ground under cultivation
   with the sun to his back
   Than a noblewoman with splendid ornaments
   Or a hero slaved to his fame

3. I wish for only one day like that sun
   Only one night like those waves
   To send a day off to meet a new day in my life
   At leisure and liberty

Written by Park Chung-Hee

Jo Gap-Je interpreted this poem as "the expression of Park's longing for things modest and unsophisticated. Park Chung-Hee has already declared that he would stand by the weak, between the weak and unsophisticated symbolized by a wild-flower and a peasant in contrast with a noblewoman and a hero."[4]

It is said that at that time Park Chung-Hee read Shim Hun's novel <*An evergreen tree*>, which was appearing serially in *Dong A-Ilbo*. It is a novel containing a story of the hero who, under Japanese imperialism, spread a movement of farm village reconstruction secretly instead of an independence movement. It seems that <*An evergreen tree*> he read in the latter half of his teens had a considerable effect on his unusual concerns about the farming population and his strong will toward recovering the scenic beauty of Korea after he became president.

Photo 20. After graduation from Daegu School of Education, he became an elementary school teacher in Mungyeong, Gyeongbuk Province.

44

First Army Headquarters Chief of Staff's Love of Trees

Park Chung-Hee met the Liberation when he graduated from the Imperial Japanese Army Academy at the end of Japanese imperialism. He entered the Korean Army Academy again, and after the Korean War, he received an official announcement of appointment as the principal of Gwangju Artillery School on October 18, 1954. The appointment was after he returned from a six-month stay in the United States for study as brigadier. As soon as he proceeded to his post, he pulled out two weeping willows standing at the entrance of the principal's office and planted pine trees there.

When lieutenant General Yu Jae-Heung, president of general headquarters of education, came for inspection and said, "It looks good." Brigadier Park responded, "Thinking that the willow's look of drooping didn't go with the spirit of soldiers, I replaced them by planting pines stretching upright." When some time later, president Yu came for inspection again, the pine trees with reddish dried leaves had been cut and left in a heap aside. When answering the question, "What happened?" Park said, "We've failed probably because the soil is not suited for pine trees." Then, President Yu said, "In the memoirs by General Douglas MacArthur, he says that a soldier knows how to cut a tree but doesn't know its physiology."[4]

In those days, there was what was called a "public welfare work" in a military unit. It corresponded with the military's irrationality, in which every unit had been engaging tacitly. Since officers received such a small salary, they used this business of lending military trucks to private traders and reaping rental fees as a means of subsidizing their livelihood. This truck would chiefly be rented by lumbering men who were felling trees in the mountains, and Principal Park publicly handed out this income to officers in an above-board manner. Sometimes the truck rental was received in firewood, at which time Principal Park piled up firewood on the drill grounds and allowed officers to take it away for heating with a set proportion of distribution. As long as his men were worried about daily meals, it seems that protection of nature was a side issue, even to Principal Park.

On July 14, 1955, the next year, General Park received an official announcement of appointment as the Fifth Division Commander. This unit was also doing the public welfare work for subsidizing officers' livelihood by felling trees in the mountains in the division's area and selling them in the rear. Although the government had set up the policy of severe punishment for illegal cutting, the persons in charge of forests in the local government were hardly ready to stop this practice because they were familiar with the circumstances of the officers receiving a pittance. They asked only that in felling trees the soldiers cut the stumps close to the ground in order not to leave a trace as a means of covering up the illegal acts. Park, divisional head, couldn't help but order cutting trees in the same manner.

What is interesting is that when later becoming president, he urged military units to participate in the reforestation project. He stressed that "military units used to damage the forests a lot, so now you ought to repay kindness by planting many trees." This way of thinking he seems to have retained from when he participated in the "public welfare work" in his military life.

In his days as a division head, Park Chung-Hee was once deeply impressed with the vitality of a tree. On his way to make a tour of inspection on each unit, he carried along a sycamore tree branch as a walking cane and stuck it someplace at random. But he accidentally passed the place and found new shoots coming out from the branch stuck upside down. This episode is known because Goh Kun, the former premier, heard it from the president when he was in charge of reforestation in the 1970s as a Saemaul counselor at the Ministry of Home Affairs. He vividly recollected that when the president laughed heartily while admiring the vitality of a sycamore tree, Goh Kun saw a snag tooth in president's mouth.

Park Chung-Hee, who was first promoted in March 1958 to major general among the second batch of the Army Academy, received an official announcement of appointment as the First Army Headquarters chief of staff on June 17 of the same year. On procession to the new post as the First Army Commander, Lieutenant General Song Yo-Chan selected Major General Park Chung-Hee. The First Army headquarters was located in Wonju and Song attached weight to external activities, entrusting the household management of the field army with Major General Park Chung-Hee.

General Song Yo-Chan, who was magnanimous and had an excellent driving force, seems to have marked Major General Park for a long time as a person he could totally entrust with internal affairs. Park Chung-Hee's careful and planning personality dovetailed with Lieutenant General Song's magnanimous and ambitious nature, so Major General Park could exercise his specialty to the full in this situation. At this period, Park, the First Army chief of staff, had two major achievements. [4]

First was the total interruption of the "public welfare work", the biggest irrationality in the history of the Korean Armed Forces. He resolutely stopped this project, even though it was difficult to eradicate. At that time, our army was composed of the First Army, a field army, and the Second Rear Army. The First Army, representing our Armed Forces, had a mighty influence on the whole of the Korean Army. As such, the First Army interrupted the public welfare work completely, which had such strong ripple effects that it caused the entire army to stop the project. It was a historical event that the soldiers' deforestation was interrupted at a breath by General Park Chung-Hee, an accomplishment that had been impossible even by the government officials to achieve. At Park's proposal of this, Song Yo-Chan was clear in his decision, too, saying, "It is nonsense that vehicles that must be used for the time of war are being scrapped for public welfare work. What if a war breaks out right now? I say, return all the vehicles to their units within thirty days."

It was the moment when a wound that had been forming puss for a decade was cut out. This way, all army trucks lent to civilians for the purpose of public welfare work were collected. It meant the end of the custom of civilians felling or illegally cutting forest trees using army trucks.

Second was a measure banning the use of firewood. At that time, most military units were using firewood for heating and cooking. Naturally, the soldiers cut down trees all year round to secure firewood. Thus, it was hardly possible to see a tree in the mountains around a military unit. In the circumstances in which the press even called the soldiers "human caterpillars," officers always had to study the pleasure of newspapermen. After the armistice, our army was all about constructing barracks, erecting positions, and construction works on tactical roads. Having to perform these construction works almost on their own, without any support of materials from outside, they had no choice but to cut trees. Commander Lee Geon-Yeong's memoir portrays the actual state of indiscriminate felling then committed by soldiers this way: [28]

"Stationing a three-quarter truck in a mountain valley, a saw was installed by pulling out the car wheel and hanging a long belt on it, and then lumbering was done instantly. An entrenching tool was sharpened, and a pick was transformed into a chisel, an ax, and an adze for the purpose of whittling and trimming the tree as an excellent lumbering tool. Spades and picks were so frequently used that they almost lost their original shape. Barbed-wire entanglements were cut out to make nails while hard biscuit bags and tobacco packs were used for papering the barracks after construction."

These things represented the actual scene of deforestation committed around military units on the front line and in the rear. It was an attempt to uproot such antinational criminal acts that Park changed fuel for heating and cooking by substituting coal for firewood.

Chapter 6. President of a Poor Country

"I Want to Take Home All of Those Green Forests!"

In May 1965, President Park visited the United States at President Johnson's invitation. After finishing many formal schedules, he visited the US Military Academy at West Point. President Park uniquely graduated from the military academies of three countries; the Manchuria Military School, the Japanese Military Academy and the Joseon Guard Academy (the former Korean Military Academy). As one who was accustomed to military culture, he enjoyed this visit very much. Several days after he left West Point, receiving the warmest farewell from Military Academy cadets, President Park said to Kim Seong-Jin, a Washington correspondent for Dongyang News Agency [17].

"Those green forests seen everywhere in the United States, I really envy them. If I were allowed to bring something back from the United States, I would want to take home all of those green forests."

Park Chung-Hee, who appreciated the green forests and the cadets' high spirits, was forty-eight years old then. During the ten years after his return from a six-month stay in 1954 in the United States for study as a brigadier general, Park hardly complimented the United States. It was really an exception when he complimented the green forests of the United States to a reporter, a subject that may have seemed trivial. In 1964, Korea's per capita income was $103, a little higher than $76 for 1961, but in 1959 statistics it was number 119 out of 120 countries around the world on the UN's list. He may have come from one of the poorest countries of the world, but when he mentioned green forests as what he was avid about, it suggested that he had a beautiful dream as president.

Photo 21. Visiting the US in May, 1965, President Park met President Johnson and promised to dispatch Korean troops to help the US, which initially fought the War of Vietnam alone.

Park Chung-Hee was a person who put substance before form with definite goals, and was straight, diligent, and thrifty. There are many anecdotes relating to this idea. When he threw out the first pitch in a baseball game, for instance, if the pitch was off course, he threw it over and again until it went through the strike zone. By nature, he couldn't forgive himself for showing 'complacency' by throwing a ball perfunctorily. He was also stern about publicizing his face. At the beginning of 1962, the year after he seized power, when he became aware that his face appeared too often on the theater news, film, and TV, he issued an order to the chief of the movie studio, Ministry of Publicity, "If there is so much film to shoot me, transfer it to making a progressive culture movie devoted to enlightening the people."[2]

On August 30, 1963, two years and three months after the military revolution, he took off his military uniform through the ceremony of discharge from military service as a full general of the army, ran in the presidential election, and was elected as the fifth president of Korea on October 15. We, forestry men tended to support Chairman Park because we saw that the revolutionary government completely finished its work straight out of policies of reforestation in just one or two years, which the past administrations just reviewed without establishing, established without enforcement, or enforced without results. We can cite exterminating the caterpillars that gnawed at the forests, doing away with illegal cutters who were called man caterpillar, planting 0.5 billion black locusts and 20 million poplars in one or two years, eradicating the carrying out of forest products by a thorough crackdown, and making the long wished-for forest law to pave the way for preservation of the country.

Photo 22. Dense forest in the United States. President Park was highly interested in mountain forests as to point out its forests as the most coveted thing he saw when he visited the US in 1965.

Temporary Act of Forest Reclamation

On February 9, 1963 before a planned fifth presidential election, the military government promulgated the "Temporary Act of Forest

Reclamation." This law, to be in effect for three years was, in a word, the one to legalize exacting statute labor. It stipulated that the Seoul Metropolitan mayor, the Busan mayor and the provincial governors should be able to mobilize compulsory labor in accordance with clauses set out in the cabinet order when considered necessary for forest reclamation. But a strict restriction was set for mobilization. The law explicitly defined Village Forestry Cooperative members for this use as people born between January 1, 1930, and December 31, 1934 (twenty-nine to thirty-three years old males then), and ones who had not been enrolled in active military service, so that participation might not affect public sentiment by compulsory mobilization. [1]

In spite of the forest-reclamation project driven by making this law using compulsory labor, it didn't work because the matter of fuel wood was not resolved yet in farm villages. In the middle of the 1960s, annual production of smokeless coal exceeded ten million tons but it was hard to carry 19-holed briquettes because there was no road open except an unpaved road to supply them to the distant rural communities. The briquettes were not actually been supplied to farm villages until roads were improved by the Saemaul Movement after 1971.

In the same year, a "fund-raising campaign for forest reclamation" was also launched. It was a private-level drive to raise funds with a little compulsory aspect stimulated by the military government's lead in reforestation, which the government assumed to be favorably accepted by the people. The Forest Cooperative Federation took the lead in raising donations against each institution and especially merrymaking places (to help overcome their negative image), which resulted in the raising of 65 million won (US $255,000) in total, and all this money was used to cover wages for workers mobilized for an erosion-control project.

As a means to save timber resources, the revolutionary government also proposed a plan to replace railroad ties and telegraph poles with concrete. It had been for these two uses that the government previously had to approve a mass felling of trees in the mountains. This policy was published after getting informed of many successful cases abroad. Though at first there was a great aversion, satisfactory results found after using a prototype led to continued replacement from then on. [1]

Illegal Cutting Incident at Mt. Jiri

About one year after the chairman of the revolutionary government Park Chung-Hee took his new office as the fifth president, there was a serious incident of illegal cutting. It was from Mt. Jiri and worth recording as number one on the scale of illegal cutting since the foundation of the country. In the summer of 1964, the Suncheon area in Jeonnam Province had great flood damage. To supply timbers for this restoration work, the state had approved legal felling of trees in about 120 ha of the forests (to harvest 9,854m³ of timber) with serious damage from pine caterpillars of the Cheoneun Buddhist temple forest and neighboring regions at Mt. Jiri. It was the largest scale of felling trees in the private forest. Taking advantage of this operation, however, illegal cutters began cutting here and there in Mt. Jiri.

In the fall of 1964, an officer in the engineer corps, who was engaged in opening an operational road in Mt. Jiri, got so angered to see the scenes of illegal cutting in so many areas that he submitted a petition to the Blue House by taking pictures of them. We need to take note how President Park dealt with this. It seemed that he considered a simple order to arrest the criminals of illegal cutting to the Ministries of Home Affairs or Agriculture and Forestry would not ensure of the eradication of such a social ill. At the beginning of October, on his inspection tour to Gwangju area, he suddenly ordered to turn the nose of his helicopter toward Mt. Jiri and verified the scene in person, and then on his arrival to Gwangju City, he immediately ordered a roundup of those involved in illegal cutting. At last, a joint search party, comprising 1,500 persons from three provinces (Jeonbuk, Jeonnam and Gyeongnam) was organized, and the National Assembly fact-finding panel formed to finalize this. Not only were man-caterpillars prevalent in Jangsu, Namwon, Gurye, and Hamyang stamped out, but many policemen, and forestry officials got arrested or dismissed from service. It must have been a shocking event to the president, but it also must have served as an opportunity to solidify his will toward reforestation.

Except for a few bad ones who wanted to make fast money by illegal cutting from mountains, most people in the country had a very low income at the time of 1964. Records indicate that female workers in a textile factory received an average monthly wage of 3,440 won (US $13.40). Looking at consumer prices at that time, registration fees of the college the author attended were 7,700 won ($30) per semester, and monthly boarding expenses were 1,400 won ($5.50). Beef for 1kg was 215 won ($0.84), ten coal briquettes 76 won ($0.29), and 20 liters of rice 736 won ($2.88). According to the survey data of the Ministry of Publicity, as of January 1964, there were domestically a total of 650,000 radio sets. Compared to the total population of 27.18 million at the end of 1963, radio penetration was 2.42 percent, meaning each village had only one radio. These statistics convince us of Korea ranking the 119th in national income among 120 countries of the world.

Photo 23. By President Park's special order, the criminals at the Mt. Jiri cutting incident were arrested wholesale by the joint investigation team of 1,500 persons.

Dense Forests in West Germany

In December 1964, President Park Chung-Hee flew to West Germany. It was the most important national event in the second year of his presidency but with a miserable aim. It was not a visit on the level of diplomacy but only for obtaining a loan. He initiated the revolution, became the chairman of the State Reconstruction Supreme Council and then president, and put his heart and soul for national reconstruction all the way, but he had no money. Though there was $110 million in aid annually from the United States, most of it was not adequate even for covering the provisions of the people. With the stark reality of spring poverty for the peasants, it was a juggling feat to fill the starving stomachs of the people and seek economic construction as well.

With his people's starvation in mind, he came forward. In the days of the military government, he tried economic construction by means of loans from abroad, but it was not easy because of low sovereignty credit and being distrusted by the United States. Considering it was impossible to obtain a loan from Anglo-American countries, he turned his eyes to Europe and started making an elaborate effort toward West Germany, a similarly divided country.

First, he sent out nurses and mine workers to West Germany. The military regime had been seeking to export manpower to earn foreign money from the start of revolution with such instructions sent to diplomatic establishments abroad. Lee Gi-Hong, a resident official in the Korean embassy in West Germany, made an inspection of many coal-mining areas. At that time, miners from Italy, Turkey, Spain, and Japan were working here, but Japanese miners tended to withdraw as their country's economic condition improved. Hearing reports of this necessity of Germany, President Park didn't hesitate. On December 21, 1963, the first team of 123 miners left for West Germany. The group sent was composed of elite personnel who had passed through repeated screenings because our high-class manpower applied en masse during a time of high unemployment. Sending miners was literally killing two birds with one stone in a win-win policy for both West Germany and Korea. Thereafter, a total of 8,395 miners were sent off.

Sending off nurses started a little earlier than that of miners. In the spring of 1960, by the arrangement of Dr. Lee Jong-Su, a Korean surgeon in the Bonn Medical School, Berlin Methodist Women Missionaries and Frankfurt Methodist Hospital admitted two nurses from Korea. Unlike the case of miners, the door was opened by a civilian. Taking this opportunity in 1962, twenty nurses got jobs in West Germany, and a total of around 1,200 nurses were sent off until 1968.

Photo 24. To President Park (age 47) visiting West Germany in December 1964, President Lubke (age 70) provided a loan as well as many political and diplomatic tips and cooperation.

From 1969, under a government initiative (Korean Overseas Development Corporation), 10,371 nurses were sent off to West Germany until 1977. It was the result of their recognizing the capability, diligence, kindness, and public spirit of Korean nurses. Especially their care for parent-like elderly patients and their nimbleness when performing their duties were recognized, while nurses learned ways of living toward order, respect for the law, thrift, saving, and faith. Of them, around a thousand nurses got married internationally on the spot and came to settle down there.

Visiting West Germany, President Park made an appeal to the parliament:

"Help us, please. We are a similarly divided country as West Germany and are confronted with a communist army. We are a sincere and reliable people. By making hard efforts, we shall definitely pay the loan back."

At last, on the security of the future three-year salaries not received by the nurses and miners yet, he was able to obtain a loan of 140 million marks (around $30 million) from Lubke, the West Germany president. In addition, President Park rushed along the Autobahn riding together with the West Germany president. Probably the Autobahn was the first and best-made highway in the world. The president from a poor country with only winding one-way single lane roads got out of the car on the way and observed the structure of the road carefully. Also, the thick forests spread on both sides of the road were a sight no less grand than the highway.

Photo 25. In his visit to West Germany, President Park met Korean nurses and miners and encouraged and rewarded them for their labors with tears rather than a speech.

Then, President Park visited the coal mine at Hamborn. It was a place where many of our miners were working, and our nurses also came running after hearing the news. In their strong homesickness, the nurses cried out loudly, holding the hem of First Lady Yook Young-Soo. The miners also wept together. On arriving at the hall, President Park was unable to make a speech because of tears coming into his eyes. They sang the national anthem together, but all being choked and their eyes being dim with tears, they only sobbed after all.

Tears Shed at the Sight of Bare Mountains in Yeongil District

West Germany is the first ranking country in reforestation, probably because it has maintained its dense forests since the beginning of the twentieth century by carrying out sustainable forest management in which it harvests timber only as much as trees grow annually. Then, how dense their forests should have been for almost a hundred years!

Seeing such dense forests, President Park admired the German people's national character that preserved the forests under difficult economic conditions as a defeated country following the First and Second World Wars, feeling strongly the potential energy of an advanced country.

The recognition of the German people's character must have rendered him added determination that as a welfare country like West Germany, growth should be preceded by reforestation as a matter of course. As if trying to make sure of his resolution, there was a queer sight evolving before President Park's eyes. It happened at the last part of President Park's return home from West Germany. His return journey was the route by way of Japan. At that time, all air flights leaving Haneda International Airport for Gimpo Airport must cross Yeongil-gun, Gyeongbuk, in a beeline. After flying over the Japanese territory with dense forests, on entering Korea's territory over the green East Sea, Korean people used to feel ashamed of the desolate picture of Yeongil-gun, which spread out just like a desert.

President Park was also suddenly faced with the reddish bare mountains of the Yeongil District after having an eyeful of the dense forests for several days in West Germany and the island country Japan as well. Heartbroken, President Park was said to have shed tears unconsciously. "It is out of the question to hoist a flag for modernizing the country over such a desolated land."[1]

Photo 26. Picture shows a wasteland in Yeongil region, Gyeongbuk, in the 1960s. President Park shed tears looking at this region from a plane on his return from West Germany and Japan, both of which have dense forests.

President Park's firm resolutions were put into action one after another. The first was a Short-Term Fuel-Wood Forest Establishment Plan, which was published one month later. As described in Part I, the Rhee Syng-Man government had started the Five-Year Fuel-Wood Forest Establishment Plan (1959-1963). However, with the project not getting off the ground properly, and the military revolution breaking out in 1961, this project was actually only succeeded for 237,000 ha by 1965.

However, President Park, thinking it would be impossible to stop illegal cutting without first ensuring a short-term fuel-wood solution, decided again to enforce a short-term establishment plan (1965-1967). At that time, gathering fallen leaves was allowed, but cutting live trees was forbidden. However, walking distances of ten or twenty ri (4 or 8 km), people cut down trees at midnight without forest ranger's monitoring in order to use it as fuel wood for cooking or heating.

Fortunately, the government had set the year of 1965 as the "Year for Work", and the Short-Term Fuel-Wood Forest Establishment Plan provided many jobs for the farming population. The government supplied corn or wheat flour in return for labor to people mobilized for making the fuel-wood forest, which was an important means of solving daily meals for families.

Goals of the fuel-wood forest

1) 1965- 1967: Added establishment of 460,000 ha
   (60,000 ha in 1965, 42,000 ha in 1966, 358,000 ha in 1967)
2) Existing fuel-wood forest: 311,000 ha
3) Transfer from the established forest to fuel-wood forest: 400,000 ha
4) Total: Planned to secure 1,171,000 ha (An area that can supply fuel for 2.5 million farmhouses around the country)

On June 10, 1965, after participating in the Farmers' Day event in Suwon, President Park visited the Institute of Forest Genetics to hear the explanation about *Populus alba* x *glandulosa* developed by Dr. Hyun Shin-Kyu (then Head of the Rural Development Administration). His breeding of a new hybrid was due to one decisive demerit in each of its parent trees, white poplar and Suwon poplar, despite their many merits. White poplar (*Populus alba*) was introduced to Korea from Europe in the latter half of the nineteenth century. With vigorous growth, good resistance to drought, and many hairs on the back side of its leaves, it is resistant to diseases and insects and roots easily from cuttings. However, since it doesn't grow up straight, it has limited value as a timber. On the other hand, the Suwon poplar (*Populus glandulosa*) adapts well to poor soil and grows up straight, while it grows slowly and is difficult to propagate by cutting.

Populus alba x *glandulosa* is a hybrid of these two tree species. Taking after the strengths of its parents, it grows quickly, has good adaptability to dry soil, grows straight up, and easily roots from cutting. It is an "upland poplar" that has also overcome the limitations of the Italian poplar, which grows well only on flat land. It also has great value as timber. President Park tried touching the *Populus alba* x *glandulosa* and encouraged planting it with many compliments. Then, *Populus alba* x *glandulosa* was spread across the country as a roadside tree and planted in large numbers, even on sloped mountainsides in secluded places. Later, this species was renamed by President Park as Hyun poplar. The highest honor bestowed upon a forest geneticist by the president was when he renamed the tree after the surname of Dr. Hyun Shin-Kyu.

Photo 27. *Populus alba* x *glandulosa* is a hybrid poplar inheriting only the strong points of its parents. It is easily propagated by cutting and strong against diseases and harmful insects. It grows fast and straight on dry mountain slopes, too. Later, President Park called it the "Hyun poplar" naming it after its developer.

Korea Institute of Science and Technology (KIST) Established in the Forest of Hongreung

In May, 1965, the same year, President Park had a summit meeting with US president Johnson and agreed to dispatch troops to Vietnam. The agreement included a clause of cooperating jointly to establish a comprehensive research institute that could contribute to the industrial development of Korea. To implement this clause as well as express gratitude for dispatching troops to Vietnam, the United States provided a special aid of $1 million. Some wanted to buy wheat flour with this money because provisions were in absolute want. But President Park ordered the establishment of the Korea Institute of Science and Technology (KIST) with $2 million by adding the aid money to Korean government contribution. In February 1966, the Foundation of Korea Institute of Science and Technology started by appointing Dr. Choi Hyeong-Seop as the first president. After looking around over thirty sites proposed in the country, Dr. Choi asked for Hongreung in the vicinity of Cheongryang-ri as the site for the institute, which was very suitable as an environment for research, with being surrounded by forests.

Hongreung is the place where Queen Myeongseong, the wife of Emperor Gojong, was buried. For Queen Myeongseong, who was murdered suddenly in 1895, it was hard to find a place for burial because the empress had to be buried together with Emperor Gojong, who was still young with no burial place designated. Unavoidably, she was buried temporarily in Hongreung until the emperor passed away. Therefore, in this place of about 120 ha, the forest was preserved so well that the Government General of Korea under Japanese occupation used this place in 1922 as Forest Experiment Station. It was being used for the same purpose after the Liberation and was fortunate enough to escape war damage during the Korean War. It seems that President Park worried a lot because scholars raised strong objections to building an institute that might damage the well-preserved forest nestling the history of the Joseon Dynasty.

In the course of inspecting the site in person in 1966, President Park explained in detail the necessity for the institute for science and technology to the Head of Rural Development Administration, resulting in the compromise of building the institute by cutting just part of the forest after all. The president felt very sorry about damaging the forest of Hongreung himself.

Then, KIST performed well above its own duty. By developing the core technology of steelmaking, the institute transferred it to Pohang Iron and Steel Company (currently, POSCO) to help it rise to the number one enterprise of steel production in the world. In the sense that the institute raised Korean industrial technology to a global level, some of the damage to the forests of Hongreung is well justified.

In October 2009, commemorating the 30th anniversary of President Park's death, chiefly scientists retired from KIST formed a friendship organization named the Yeonwoo Society and had their first meeting for building the "Park Chung-Hee Science and Technology Memorial Hall". It was an occasion for officially recognizing that President Park's pioneering ideas of "prosperity of a nation on the basis of industries" made a great contribution to developing Korea's current science and economy.

Even though the institute damaged the Hongreung forest initially, stock volume for forests across the country grew from 9.2m^3/ha in 1966 when KIST was established to 126m^3/ha, an over tenfold increase, 44 years later, according to statistics of the Forest Service for 2010. President Park has realized the prosperity of a nation, not only through industry but by forestry as well.

Part 3.

Launch of the Forest Service

Chapter 7. Another Year of Take-off, 1967

Initiation of the Forest Service

Looking back, the year 1967 was a very unusual one. The most extreme drought in seventy years caused damages to 400,000 ha of farmland and affected 660,000 farmhouses. Of 870,000kw generating facilities, water-power generation equivalent of 220,000kw all but stopped. However, when it came to conservation of Korean rivers and forests, 1967 was a year of revolution.

First, the Forest Bureau under the Ministry of Agriculture and Forestry was promoted in status to the Forest Service, second, fuel-wood forest establishment was resumed, and third, slash-and-burn farming regulation project was started. Also happening this year was the determination of the watershed forest-reclamation project, the enforcement of erosion control at Woi-dong, Gyeongbuk, the designation of the first national park, the groundbreaking of the Soyang-River multipurpose dam, the publication of the proposed construction of the Seoul-Busan expressway, and the groundbreaking of Pohang Iron and Steel, Inc (later POSCO).

This list included over ten major projects or policies, all of which were the most coveted projects for this country for a decade or a century. In addition, at that time, there were waves of opposition to a few projects. In spite of that, however, each of these gigantic projects for conserving rivers and forests were perfectly completed, leaving nothing to be desired. As far as conservation of rivers and forests, years like 1967 and 1973, the latter of which will be discussed in Part 4, will never come again.

Photo 28. Opening of the office in January 1967, pursuant to establishment of the Forest Service. It denotes the government's intention to drive forward forest reclamation earnestly.

Economists agree upon regarding 1967 as the first year of Korea's take-off stage. It is because this year we started the construction of POSCO and our exports broke the record of $300 million. This figure has great meaning. In 1960, the previous year of the military revolution, we received a total of $240 million in aid from abroad, but at last we earned foreign currency of more value than the aid on our own. This situation is easy to understand by recollecting that at that time our country, suffering from the spring austerity, couldn't have escaped a successive occurrence of deaths from hunger without aid from the United States.

In the author's eyes, President Park's I-can-do leadership enabled the revolution of conserving rivers and forests in just six years after the military revolution and caused the first stage of take-off (the Industrial Revolution?). The second stage of take-off noted by economists is 1970. It is because this year saw the achievement of $1 billion in exports, a 330 percent increase in exports in just three years. It is said that the third year of take-off is 1977, which resulted in an export volume of $10 billion, a 1,000 percent increase over the GNI of seven years before, possibly an isolated case in the world history of exports increase. Through the eighteen years of its regime, President Park Chung-Hee increased the exports 448 times. In 1979, the last year of his regime, the

Korean people exported $14.7 billion, recording 42.8 percent annual exports growth, reckoning from the first year of his taking power.

The year of 1967 was the first year of the Second Five-Year Economic Development Plan (1967-1971), which, in a word, was the program designed to get the people out of hunger by securing food as much as necessary. But this also included the forest rehabilitation plan and the short-term fuel-wood forest establishment plan. The underlying concept was that the first purpose of self-sufficiency of food of the Five-Year Economic Development Plan should go abreast with forest reclamation, such as the erosion-control project and the short-term establishment of fuel-wood forests. It was probably this kind of solid economic development plan that brought forth results of a satisfactory level.

The Forest Service was newly established on January 1, 1967. There were 176 personnel disposed, which, with the addition of 412 people in forest protection positions for each city and province, scaled up into a total of 588 persons. Though from the days under the Ministry of Agriculture and Forestry, the Forest Bureau had reported its duties directly to the president, it was one of the few institutions that directly reported to the president along with the Korean CIA, even after its independence from the Ministry of Agriculture and Forestry. This enables us to surmise the degree of the president's interest in forest reclamation.

Photo 29. The high-school girls who participated in the tree planting during the 1960s must have come to appreciate the dense forest later on.

It seems that when the Arbor Day was nearing in 1967, President Park thought that officials under him were failing to read his mind on forest reclamation. For President Park sent pressing personal messages on the background of newly establishing the Forest Service and restoring the green rivers and forests to the mayors, county headmen, and heads of related institutions, as noted in *<Forest Protection>*, April 1967 issue.

"I have long believed that recovering the green picture of our country's landscape is the shortest way to reconstruct and modernize our fatherland. I became even firmer in such beliefs when I witnessed in my many visits to our friendly nations the fact that the green mountains are in direct proportion to the affluence of society. That, of my will, led to first establishing the Forest Service, and then this year we are planning by creating substantial budget without precedence to plant 1.7 billion trees in 466,000 ha of mountain area, which is a project nearly four times the scale of an average year.......

In the same year, President Park expressed his concern for reforestation in his radio speech for the sixth presidential election, too:

"I pledge before our people that I shall be a president working on the spot.............I will lead the reforestation of mountain areas myself............ So I will go about anything that can be of help to our people's independence to shorten the path to self-reliance. "

Photo 30. In the spring, short of hands and equipment, the government mobilized soldiers to assist in the reforestation project.

Such a campaign speech of President Park was not merely lip service. In his presidency, he appeared on every spot of interest and was a ruler who never determined his plan without looking around the spot first. When Park was commander of artillery for the third Army Corps, he scolded officers under his command: "Nothing can be done when you work with ears and mouth. You should work with legs and eyes. Order is 5 percent and supervision and check are 95 percent." His directive to the officers shows his initiative in his work.

It was on April 15 of the same year that the Soyang River, Gangwon-do, had a ground-breaking ceremony for its multipurpose dam. This dam, with a 1.9 billion ton water storage capacity is still the largest in Korea and makes a great contribution to many fields of industry, including prevention of floods and water-power generation. Realizing the necessity of this dam early, President Park hurried its building. He set a limitation on mountain-type Gangwon-do as a reserve for a catchment area in time for supplying drinking water to rapidly increasing residents in the metropolitan areas. He also issued an order to take action to devise plans of reforesting Gangwon-do early to raise its capacity for storing water. These days over twenty-two million people (about 45 percent of the total population) are residing in Seoul, the Capital city, and its surrounding Gyeonggi-do. Gangwon-do is mostly responsible for supplying city water for them.

Five-Year Fuel-Wood Forest Establishment Plan

The year 1967, which saw the start of the Forest Service, set the record of making the fuel-wood forest on the largest scale in history. Of course, it was not that the whole forest was completed within the same year. A large-scale reforestation was only possible in 1967 because in the autumn of 1965 sufficient seeds had already been collected, and nurseries finished raising the planting stocks in 1966. Anyway, in 1967, the government finished planting 1.44 billion seedlings on 364,000 ha, spending a budget of 130 million won (US $478,000), which was in excessive of 5,766 ha compared with the area planned for. Tree species for making the fuel-wood forest included black locust (40 percent), pitch pine (40 percent), alders and others (20 percent). It was interpreted at that time that initiation of the Forest Service had sparked a new start by mobilizing all the staff of the Forestry Cooperative. In this process, the government bore the burden for seedlings, fertilizer, and reforestation training tuition, supplying aid grains from the United States (Public Law 480) to Village Forestry Cooperative members mobilized into labor force.

However, there were problems, too. The start of the Forest Service in 1967, in conjunction with the establishment of the fuel-wood forest, was too ambitious a plan to avoid some trial and error. It was just a result of the enforcement of an impractical plan. First, the fuel-wood forest was in principle to be made up autonomously by the residents in accordance with the Forestry Cooperative, unlike the general reforestation, which was led by the state. There were about 21,000 villages across the country, with one Gun (county) comprising an average of 140 villages. But there were about ten reforestation guides for each county who gave guidance to as many as 140 villages. Besides, there were cases of failing to acquire seedlings in time. In such circumstances, some one-year-old seedlings of small size were planted out to the mountains instead.

Learning from such problems, the Forest Service reestablished the Five-Year Fuel-wood Forest Establishment Plan from 1968 to 1971 with an annual target of 150,000 ha. To raise 1.4 billion plants a year, rice paddies were used for village tree nurseries, with the government allocating the number of seedlings to be produced and funded in each village. Since the tree nursery project had proceeded in Korea from the 1948 establishment of the government, the technology was already available to the farmers.

In carrying out the reforestation project, the procedure followed what the government had set, but enforcement was under the charge of the local Forest Cooperative organizations around the country. When the Village Forestry Cooperative agreed on projects, the county Forest Cooperative determined needed areas, plant species, and sites. The central government provided seedlings and fertilizers for free, while local government paid the cost of freight. The Forest Cooperative provided technology, while the Village Forest Cooperative planted trees by mobilizing free labor and taking charge of post-management.

In addition, the Village Forest Cooperative also participated in "proxy execution". Even though mountain lands surrounding the village were mostly privately owned, the government would issue to the land owners orders to plant trees according to the Forest Law. If the land owner failed to respond, the government had the local village forest cooperative carry out the project by proxy. After planting trees, the government charged the expenses for proxy execution to the owner of the land. If the land owner failed to respond, it was considered according to the forest law that the "shared income" contract was closed; 80 to 20 percent between Village Forest cooperative and the land owner, respectively. The "Shared income" means sharing profit gained after reforestation. It was a most welcome transaction for the land owner because he could receive 20 percent of the profit by doing nothing, while the land became more fertile and was stocked with trees.

For a successful tree nursery project, gathering seeds is important. The government purchased seeds in cash while all village people assiduously participated in gathering and selling seeds of black locust, alder, and Lespedeza. There being many farmhouses starving then, gathering seeds was well received, even by children's participation, providing a good means of earning money, though in small amounts. At that time "wild seeds" were used because it was before the concept of "improved seeds" was introduced by breeding, which took many years of scientific research. Thus, using wild seeds was considered a timely decision for the short-term, fast-growing trees for the fuel-wood forest.

Photo 31. Gathering seeds, a basic necessity of the tree nursery, doesn't take complex techniques, but many helping hands. Even elementary school students participated in the state's project and earned pocket money for their families.

In those days, the fervor of planting trees for making the fuel-wood forest was great. Village people gathered from early in the morning because the right to gather fuel from this fuel-wood forest was given to a household, with one person participating in this compulsory labor. While the father kept busy working in the farming season, even a thirteen-year-old child could come forward to carry the seedlings on his back. This compulsory labor was a job without pay, so there was usually no compensation in wheat flour. However, when more than one person from a household participated, a gourd bowl of wheat flour was provided for a half-day's work. The major tree species for fuel-wood forest was the black locust. Planting this species did not require digging a hole in advance. But a chestnut tree or an apricot tree must have a large hole dug in advance.

In general reforestation, there was a daily allowance given, so all came forward to plant trees in the days of scarce provisions and hardly any means to make money. Grandpa, grandma, and married women all were able to receive daily allowances, and even thirteen-year-old children were allowed a wage half the grownups'. Sometimes, one's work for a week gathered was given in wheat or corn flour or at other times in cash. In southern areas, this project usually started on March 1, and the planting period ended no later than April 20. With the end of planting period, youths engaged in an exchange of farming labor or looked around a river erosion-control site for other jobs, while experienced persons could be employed on a long-term basis at the mountain erosion-control site. [1]

The fact-finding survey on the fuel-wood forest established this way was carried out in 1972. Of the 784,000 ha total area of finished reforestation, it was verified that only 435,000 ha remained, reflecting the result that about half of the reforestation area survived. At that time, the die off of trees was ascribed to changes into other land use and the immature technology of reforestation.

The Erosion-Control Project Forms the Groundwork for Forest Rehabilitation

Now, let's discuss the erosion-control project. A bare mountain will be washed away, dug up, and torn down by even a small amount of rain. The Erosion-control project intends to fix earth and make drainage arrangements. It began earnestly in 1967. Titled "the Watershed Forest Reclamation Plan" (1967-1976), this project expended 10 billion won (US $36.8million) for a total of 65,030 ha and was carried out in its latter part in connection to the "First Ten-Year Forest Rehabilitation Plan" of 1973.

To be noted is the Woi-dong region's erosion-control project in Gyeongbuk province that began in September, 1967. Being a different place from Yeongil region (4,500 ha) which had caused President Park to shed tears on his return journey in 1964, the Woi-dong region was around 500 ha of waste-land that could threaten the Ulsan industrial complex in the event of a large-scale landslide. On his return to Seoul by train after an inspection of Ulsan industrial complex in the summer of 1967, President Park sent his signed instructions to Yang Taek-Shik, then the Gyeongbuk province governor: "Going by train about one kilometer toward Ulsan from Weolseong county Ipshil Station, you will see mountains with a very poor state of erosion control on the east side." In this instruction, he advised, "It is a steep mountain in a rocky area by nature, and an ordinary method of erosion control will not do because the soil will be washed away, and grasses and trees won't survive well. So it will take technology of a special method of construction." He recorded in detail, "I hope for your prompt start within the end of this year, if possible, so that people in the future may exclaim how the poor mountains have been so wonderfully reclaimed." [7]

The Woi-dong region in the neighborhood of Gyeongju, Gyeongbuk, is an upper stream of the Taehwa River running to Ulsan Port (Ulsan Industrial Complex) and on the west of Mt. Dongdae. Mt. Dongdae has a very steep slope and sandy soil ready to wash out because of weathering of its granite. It had remained as a sole vacant land amounting to 498 ha for such a long time. Before the Liberation in 1945, and then several times until 1966, erosion-control projects for this region had been executed for a total floor area of 2,820 ha, but all failed.

Under these circumstances, with participation by military units as well as the provinces and counties, in a tragic but brave resolution, the erosion-control project started again in September 1967. Between September and June the next year, officials executed groundwork for the mountain area (250 ha), sowing seeds (250 ha), repairing the existing erosion control sites (100 ha), fertilizing (70 ha), and controlling torrent erosion for the river. Applying special erosion-control methods of construction, engineers made horizontal terraces, added fertile soil brought from another place and attempted early greening by planting five-year-old black pines. [8]

Photo 32. This stretch of bare mountain pours down enough soil to transform the topography of the neighboring area in a single big rain. The Erosion-control project started earnestly in 1967 when the Forest Service was established.

Laborers mobilized at that time numbered from one thousand to two thousand people a day, and officials in charge of technological guidance could hardly go back home, even on weekends, for nine months at a time. This way, tasks for half a century were resolved in nine months. It was the result of the president's special concern, combined with governor Yang Taek-Shik's enthusiasm. [32]

There is one thing, though seemingly insignificant, that cannot be overlooked: the establishment of the forestry fund in the 1967 special accounting of financial funds operation. It was a measure for loaning mid-term financial funds to ardent foresters. Another thing is the separate order by President Park to execute the budget short for the fuel-wood forest project by special assignment out of the reserve fund. This suggests the president's strong will toward implementing the planned tree-planting project.

Photo 33. In an erosion-control project, the basic idea is to make a terrace on which to plant trees, with all the work done manually because putting equipment in is impossible.

In 1967, tree planting for the Seoul metropolitan area actively evolved. Mountains around the city, including Mt. Bukhan, Gwanak and Inwang (where the Blue House was located), were mostly bare. Tree planting was executed on a total 120 ha of mountains. The project even mobilized high school girls. Additionally, for 109 ha of desolate mountains and forests near Yeongdeungpo-gu and Gupabal, erosion control was performed by planting 250,000 trees of improved poplar, black locust, white pine, and larch. This project involved 3.2 tons of fertilizer and 1,800 total man-days.

Another important project was enforced in 1967 when the Forest Service started. It is the Slash-and-Burn Farming Regulation Project with the relevant law enacted a year earlier in 1966. The slash-and-burn farming means a way of illegally cultivating mountainous lands after burning down the forest. January 20 to July 20, 1967 were set as voluntary reporting periods for slash-and-burn fields. Reports on Gangwon, Chungbuk, Gyeongbuk and Gyeongnam were received involving a total of 51,424 ha. For some reason, the slash-and-burn farming regulation doesn't seem to have proceeded actively after 1967. In 1973, however, when Forest Service moved under the Ministry of Home Affairs, it resumed at full scale until, at last in 1979, all slash-and-burn fields in our country disappeared.

Photo 34. Women also helped in reforestation and the erosion-control project by taking unusually rough work, such as carrying earth in plastic bowls on their heads.

During the autumn of 1967, a welcome piece of news came to the Blue House. It was the first export of pine mushrooms to Japan. Japanese people count pine mushrooms as one of their favorite foods. This occurred when Japan's domestic output of pine mushrooms was decreasing because its pine forests were thickening too much. International flights opened by normalization of diplomatic relations between the two countries established a system of directly sending fresh pine mushrooms by air from Korea. Pine mushrooms reaped from Gangwon, Chungbuk, and Gyeongbuk provinces were collected by the Forestry Cooperative, delivered to Seoul in a truck over-night, sent to Tokyo by the first plane the next morning, and were displayed in downtown stores in the afternoon. It was a speed game in which it took less than twenty-four hours from harvest to arrival at the market.

In the first year, 1967, 28 tons of pine mushrooms were exported, earning only the equivalent of US $60,000, but soon exports increased to 887 tons for $25.8 million by 1978. Pine mushrooms were by that point the item that contributed most to export totals. Then, the pine mushrooms became precious, with a steady increase of exports, and in 1992, 749 tons were exported for record $81.6 million. More recently, with the domestic demand for pine mushrooms increasing, exports to Japan are rapidly decreasing.

Designation of the First National Park

Another big step for conservation of our country's mountains and forests was the designation of the first national park on December 19, 1967. The Natural Park Act, a ground law for designation of a national park, is very strict. It even bans simple cooking or turning on a portable burner to make coffee within the boundaries of a national park. It is clear why the government introduced the national park system. It is to contribute to improving the health, refreshment, and minds of the people by protecting natural landscapes and seeking a proper level of use. The first national park designated in 1967 was Mt. Jiri. (The reason Mt. Jiri was chosen will become apparent in the second part of this book <President of a Poor Country>.)

Mt. Jiri National Park includes 47,176 ha of mountains and includes one city, four counties, and seventeen eups and myeons (township). Mt. Jiri is a place known as the holy ground for the national faith, and it is honored by the people as one of the three god-like mountains (along with Mt. Geumgang and Mt. Halla). It has two dozen peaks over 1,500 meters high and is focused on three major peaks like a folding screen covered with clouds and mist and mystery, boasting its magnificent figure, encompassing the three provinces of Jeonnam, Jeonbuk and Gyeongnam.

When an area is designated as a national park, some degree of development is made for access roads and amenities, with some expected damage by visitors. However, fundamentally, construction and development are strictly limited within the designated zone, which decisively protects the God-given nature. By controlling artificial reforestation in the district, it is possible to preserve and add to the already well-established existing forests, thus creating a more beautiful natural forest.

Early in the project of designating Mt. Jiri as a national park, three provinces surrounding Mt. Jiri competed for the location of the gateway to the park. The decision was not easy to make, so President Park conducted a field investigation in person. As a result, the gateway was installed at Sa-ri, Sancheong-gun, Gyeongnam.

Photo 35. Starting with Mt. Jiri National Park in 1967, President Park designated thirteen national parks during his time in power. The picture shows the present aspect of Mt. Juwang National Park, designated in 1976.

At the times of President Park's death in 1979, a total of thirteen national parks had been designated. Since then eight national parks were added, the most recent being Mt. Mudeungsan National Park, which was designated in 2012. This national park system was introduced early in the 1960s, and it is estimated to have contributed greatly to preserving nature's gift and protecting Korea's beautiful forests. We can hardly deny that we owe this pleasant gift to a perspicacious national leader.

Chapter 8. Multiple Uses of Mountains and Forests

Year of Developing Multiple-Use Forests

President Park declared the year 1968 as "the year for developing multiple-use forests". The concept of multiple-use forests was a kind of new idea discussed at an international conference held in Seattle, Washington, USA, in 1960. He was advised by the Forest Service that multiple-use forests would promote better utilization of mountain forest area (for example, forest recreation, wildlife protection, and stockbreeding in addition to wood production), which occupy two-thirds of the land.

President Park applied this new concept to promote income from the forests, and contributed many useful trees to farm villages. Whenever the young trees of poplar, chestnut, and common apricot, bestowed by the president arrived in villages, the population clamored as if some big, promising event occurred. This was especially true when chestnut trees were expected. Villagers would dig a hole around one meter in diameter beforehand. Thinking that chestnut trees would help to solve the food problem, President Park advised this step right after the revolution that brought him to power. The trees bestowed by the president usually were delivered by an army truck, and sometimes soldiers participated in the planting. Grafting techniques were also taught.

The Forest Service also actively established public relations activities in tree-planting project. Using the slogan "Let's plant the nation's green hope in the mountain", the Forest Service encouraged people nationwide to participate in the tree-planting project through messages on cigarette packs, on stamps, and in radio broadcasts. In preparation for the national tree-planting period, the Forest Service strengthened forest-fire prevention campaigns, and installed reforestation poles on the slash-and-burn fields, forest patrol boxes, and forest-fire watchtowers. It also constructed barracks to house officials who would monitor illegal cutting.

Photo 36. Kim Hyun Ok, Minister of Home Affairs, emphasized that planting a tree is the way to love our country through the slogan "Let's go to a mountain singing the national anthem".

Every spring, the Forest Service's tree-planting posters reading "Let's go to the mountain'" fluttered in every corner of village entrances. On tree-planting days, students went to school carrying a pick or spade with them. During such days, school shortened their hours, and students went to the mountains dreaming about another Dalgas (1828-1894, a Danish pioneer who planted trees by cultivating waste-land) and carrying packed lunches of pressed down boiled barley or rice combined with soy bean paste and sliced vegetables preserved in soy sauce as a side dish [1]. There was also the tree-planting to commemorate troops being sent to Vietnam. Soldiers who received a dispatch order to Vietnam participated in the reforestation project in remembrance before leaving the country.

Photo 37. Bam Island in the Han River, Seoul, which had been a target of civil efforts, became the paradise for migratory birds in no time after the 1968 reforestation.

When a truck with a huge load of tree seedlings entered a village, it had to be unloaded soon and covered with a straw mat or temporarily planted for "heeling-in". When the fertilizer arrived the next day, it was put in the village storehouse. Villagers had to carry out tasks such as maintaining reserved land for planting, managing a nursery, digging seedlings out, making boxes for packing and transporting, with great speed. Youths worked hard to find a job for the entire spring to earn the least amount of provisions they needed. In those days, planting trees in the mountains was the highest paying job in a farm village.

However, there was also a shadow over this system. Wages of the laborers were just about half the average wage, and even that was supplied in the form of about 3 kg of wheat flour or corn per person, which helped considerably resolve the matter of food in the spring austerity period. The funds came until 1967 from "PL480", the US State Department's plan for supporting food efforts in the world's poorest countries while technical support came from ICA.

Too often, heartrending pictures of peasants mobilized for a tree-planting project were also seen. Since there were few households that could afford to eat the three whole meals a day, at lunch breaks workers tended to divide into two groups; those who really brought lunch and those who only pretended to eat by unpacking an empty lunch box and staying far apart. Gathering together in the afternoon, however, all would appease their hunger by planting trees diligently [1]. Without their humiliation, patience, and perspiration, there wouldn't be green mountains today. The author bows his head with reverence to Korea's senior people, who have handed rich life down to us.

Also, we should definitely remember the devotion of the Forest Service personnel in those days. The Forest Service officials working under President Park were devoted to their duties wholeheartedly because they knew of the president's confidence in them and because it was most rewarding that the policies they created were being enacted to serve the country. Despite the fact that President Park was a taciturn and dispassionate man, many forestry officials respected him because he was an upright president, and his habit of noticing their assiduity won their hearts.

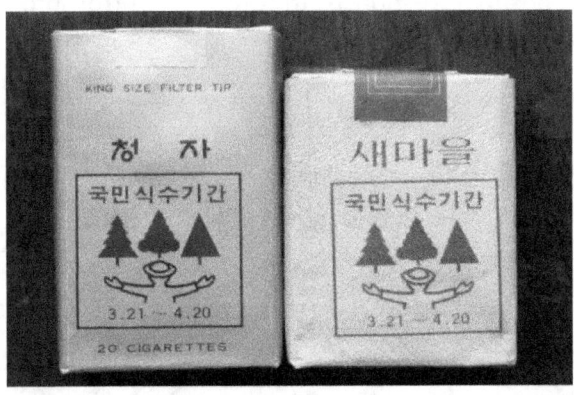

Photo 38. In those days, most men enjoyed smoking and people who remember this pack of cigarettes must have reached an old age. The forest reclamation project was an all-out publicity war.

At that time, forestry people worked until late, returning to the office after finishing the supervision of the planting site. They exchanged jokes about turning blackish in the face because they had jajangmyeon (a kind of noodle with black topping) so often. The forest officials were equally busy. When supervision of tree-planting was finished in the spring, they had to perform myriad tasks, such as guarding the survival of the planted trees by preventing diseases and insects. For transportation, only a bike or rarely a motorcycle was available to forest officials. One jeep was designated to the head of Regional Forest Office.

This year, the first-ever seed orchard in the history of Korea was established. Under a proposal by Dr. Hyun Shin-Kyu, founder of the Institute of Forest Genetics, the first such institute in the Orient, selective breeding began to improve seeds for forest tree species. Selective breeding was the global trend then, and superior individual trees growing wild in the forest were selected to be planted in the seed orchard.

There are other noteworthy things in such reforestation and tree-planting projects. First, in these reforestation and erosion control projects, a large number of residents got together to improve farm life. This work included improvement of furnaces, maintenance of the village road, and cleaning of the village. Naturally these efforts created a sense of cooperation among the village people, which served as the basis for Saemaul Movement to begin. Second, as continued reforestation and erosion-control projects gradually decreased flood damage, the farming population's positive response to erosion-control projects became noticeably higher.

Photo 39. When the red, bare, exposed soil begins to disappear under green here and there, you can be sure that reforestation has succeeded. This picture illustrates successful reforestation in Muju, Jeonbuk.

The First Year of Promoting Stockbreeding

The year 1968 was the first year for promoting stockbreeding. President Park, who had been racking his brains on "how to enable our people to drink milk" seems to have decided that it was about time to "make money by breeding cows." On Farmer's Day, June 10, he ordered Lee Gye-Sun, Minister of Agriculture and Forestry, to "develop mountainous districts to promote stockbreeding. Since our farming is focused on rice and barley, isn't it too sensitive to drought and flood damage? So find ways of diversifying the land use by stockbreeding to boost farmers' income."

In September 1968, President Park made formal visits to Australia and New Zealand with an aim to learn from examples of advanced countries for promoting a domestic stockbreeding industry and to close a bilateral technical agreement for developing groundwater and pasturage. In the summit meeting with John Gorton (1911-2002), Australian premier, the two countries reached an agreement on stockbreeding, forestry, fishery and culture. In the field of forestry, it was agreed that Korea would receive equipment and experiment instruments for a 1968-forest soil survey project by means of Colombo Plan (Cooperative Economic and Social Development in Asia and the Pacific).

In 1969, the government made the Pasture Law, which launched a large-scale pasture-making project through forest clearing. Enterprise stock farms formed in Daegwalryeong, Gangwon-do, Bukjeju-gun, Jeju-do, and elsewhere. In this way, 196 stockbreeding complexes were established around the country over three years. A nation-wide stockbreeding boom occurred. This is why 1968 is recorded as the first year of Korea's promotion of stockbreeding.

Another plan involved set-up of large-scale stockbreeding complex. The farming population took this opportunity and tried to clear and transfer mountain areas into stock farms. Naturally, those involved in forestry voiced concerns, because they feared that clearing reforested mountains might again leave the mountains bare. Fortunately or unfortunately, however, the large-scale stockbreeding complex project ended in failure, because disputes arose between stock farm owners and residents about the distribution of calves. As a result, large-scale destruction of forests was avoided. Nonetheless, the stockbreeding effort opened the way toward the mass production of milk.

After returning from Australia, President Park ordered Kim Yeong-Jin, head of the Forest Service, to take a look at the effective reforestation efforts in Australia and New Zealand and then to drive forward with a new policy. In November 1968, Kim Yeong-Jin visited Australia and New Zealand to inspect their artificial plantations. Soon after he finished the tour, Kim Yeong-Jin ordered development of a "large-complex (timber tree) reforestation plan". In Korea this was the first time government planned to make an unified large-scale reforestation complex that would bring state, public, and private forests together.

Through the "forest land use classification survey", the Forest Service searched for suitable locations for reforestation. Fourteen complexes were established. It was a plan to secure 310,000 ha of timber forest within five years and to continue for thirty-five years thereafter. The tree species selected included white pine, larch, Geumgang pine, and fir, and, for southern region, Sugi and Hinoki. Special-use trees (nut trees) included chestnut, walnut and persimmon. At this point, the existing forest-rehabilitation project focusing on fuel-wood forest began to refocus on timber trees. At the beginning of the new project, reforestation went smoothly. However, it appeared that this new project did not continue after the Forest Service was transferred to Ministry of Home Affairs in 1973, when the Forest Service dramatically changed the direction of the reforestation plan.

As noted earlier, 1967 was the "year of another take-off", meaning that 1967 witnessed numerous tree-planting and related projects. However, many projects were carried out in 1968 and 1969 as well. And they were not restricted to tree-planting projects. Let's review just a few of the major projects. In July 1969, the Gyeongin Expressway was opened, while Kim Hyun-Ok, Seoul mayor, started to build a new town for Seoul. "New Seoul city" was a new concept. At that time, Seoul was limited to the area north of the Han River. The new project began development of the area to the south which until then consisted mostly of rice paddies, dry fields and orchards, as well as the Yeouido area by building additional bridges over the Han River. It was really a historic year.

In the latter half of the 1960s, President Park began to build an expressway, which some people laughed at because, they said, it wasn't needed for our small country. Yet he persevered. Going further, he even proposed making an automobile. It is natural that we should need an automobile since cars and roads are inseparably related to each other. However, the industry leaders were alarmed to hear the president's plan for producing automobiles. They dismissed the proposal by saying, "the president is leading the way to the point of being insensible". The president had predicted that Korea would eventually have "one car for one family". But no one was ready to accept this prediction as true. To me, I was attending a college at the time, these words didn't sound real at all. In 1979, when I returned home after study in the United States, the prediction still seemed like something far in the future. My doubt was understandable after all, since it took another two full years before I even got a phone installed in my home, never mind getting an automobile!

Introduction of the Historical Greenbelt System

The year of 1971 was also a historic one. A dramatic policy was established that would preserve the forests and create green zones in our cities. This policy was originally introduced by President Park to influence urban planning. Nevertheless, many of today's forestry people believe that the policy played a decisive role in preserving mountain forests around cities. As industrialization proceeded from the 1960s, the populations of large Korean cities including Seoul, began to increase rapidly. Expansion of cities was disorderly, and it was damaging the surrounding forests during the latter part of the 1960s.

The city of London in the United Kingdom introduced the first greenbelt system in 1938. The system was designed to preserve the forests around the city for the long term. After Canada designated Ottawa as its new Capital in 1950, it also adopted a greenbelt system to preserve nearby forests. Despite the fact that there was no Korean expert on greenbelts during the 1960s, President Park wanted to establish such a system early enough to preserve the forests and green areas around Korea's cities. Even now, because preserving undeveloped area can suppress the land values, such policies are considered a suitable land use planning strategy during the early stages of development in developing countries. Many parties were affected by the policy in Korea, so there were serious disagreements, but many favored the policy, too.

In 1968, while Kim Hyun-Ok, Seoul mayor, was pushing for expanding the city like a bulldozer by developing Gangnam, President Park issued an order to Secretary Dong Hun to devise "a plan for checking the concentration of population in the metropolitan area." Presenting many plans, Secretary Dong Hun lightly mentioned the UK's greenbelt system simply for reference. Yet President Park instantly expressed his interest and adopted this system. [6]

Photo 40. Seoul, a city with a population of 11 million, is famed as a city in good harmony with nature. It achieved this harmony, in part, by securing a green zone with the greenbelt system at the beginning of the 1970s. The picture shows Mt. Nam and the green zone in the vicinity that occupies the center of Seoul (photo courtesy of City of Seoul).

At last, at the beginning of 1971, the government amended the City Planning and Zoning Act as the basis for establishing a limited development district (greenbelt). In July 1971, the first greenbelt was officially announced in the capital city, Seoul, followed by Busan and other metropolitan areas. In 1973 the policy expanded to the whole country, including Jeju Island. Greenbelts were designated for seven metropolitan areas and seven medium-size city areas, while also ensuring that the forests in the region were preserved. By the year of 1977, 5.4% of total land area were designated as greenbelt by President Park.

Since then, this greenbelt system has been challenged by civil appeals, which are filed incessantly each time power changes, and some areas have been released as sites for urgent public works. Still, it has been invaluable for ensuring that the mountains around the metropolitan cities remain green. It will be up to future historians to assess how big an influence the National Territory Use Management Act, enacted under the Yushin constitution, has on citizens' exercise of property rights.

"It is almost a miracle that Korea has succeeded in its greenbelt policy." Professor Bae Cheong has said. Without President Park's foresight and passion about greenbelts, we would have been living among endlessly spreading buildings, as we see in Tokyo, Japan today. We would not have been able to protect Seoul with such beauty and thick forests.[24]

Chapter 9. Battle in Yeongil District

The President's Memory

Some anecdotes tell of President Park's special interest and amazing memory about nature and forests. In one such story, President Park participated in the March 1971 graduation ceremony of the Army Academy. After the ceremony, while walking to the headquarters building with the principal, Lieutenant General, Choi Se-In, President Park said casually, "General Choi, the pines at the academy bear many cones. It looks like many children in a poor farm house."

As soon as the president left, Lieutenant Choi called Kim Jun-Bong, commanding officer, and issued an order to pick all the cones off all the pines at the Army Academy. The work was finished with the support of one battalion of military prisoners at Namhansanseong together with military policemen. A year later, the president again participated in the graduation ceremony. As in the previous year, after the ceremony he walked to the school headquarters with the principal. The president, looking right and left, said, "General Choi, you've picked off all the cones." According to the record, Kim Jun-Bong, who overheard the remark, was speechless at the amazing memory of the president. The story shows that President Park had tremendous interest in trees and forests.

Sohn Soo-Ik, Gyeonggi-do governor (later head of Forest Service), recalls a similar experience. Seven willow trees had been planted in front of a village on Seoul-Busan Expressway, Yongin-gun, Gyeonggi-do. In the summer of 1972, because of a storm and flood damage, two of the trees fell down. One had to be cut completely, the other was saved through the use of a prop to keep it right. One day, President Park visited the provincial office. When he got out of his car, he asked Governor, Sohn "I saw there was one tree lost in front of the village. What happened?" Governor Son recollected that he was stunned and felt awe that President Park knew the national territory like his backyard. He also felt amazed at having witnessed this part of the president's character that never neglected even the most minute part of anything in his care.

"Defend the Ulsan Industrial Complex."

President Park's tenacity on forest rehabilitation was evident during the process of driving the erosion-control project. The examples of Ulju-gun, Gyeongnam, and Yeongil District, Gyeongbuk provide a record. [1] On July 26, 1972, Typhoon Rita hit the southern part of the Korean Peninsula. Then, from September 3 to 14, a localized, torrential downpour of 213 mm caused a landslide. After the storm, fifty-four people were dead or missing.

Photo 41. In erosion-control work, part of a mountain cut and scooped out should be filled by bringing earth from another place in order to allow grass and trees to grow. Such work must rely 100 percent on A-frames carried by people working like ants that bite and carry their food to its destination.

On September 16, President Park and Kim Hyun-Ok, Minister of Home Affairs, found the cause of the landslide in an inspection of the site by helicopter. They saw that two places in the peak of the back mountain at Ehwa Village, Jungsan-ri, Neungso-myeon, Ulju-gun, Gyeongnam, had an abrupt cut where the earth had come down and formed a sheer precipice. Additional landslides were feared. Earth and sand could flow into Ulsan Bay, gateway to Ulsan Industrial Complex, and close down the harbor. The president personally devised a plan for blocking an additional landslide. He ordered that concrete be placed on the precipice. The concrete was to be bound up with an iron rope, a concrete pile driven into the lower end, and the slope stabilized by putting a breast wall around it.

Subsequently, he created a special erosion-control project group for the Ulju-gun landslide. The group included Gyeongnam deputy governor as head, Gyeongbuk Provincial Office Construction director as chief technician. By special order of Kim Hyun Ok, Minister of Home Affairs, Goh Kun Saemaul Movement director (later prime minister) established a headquarters on the site and presided over a meeting. Hurriedly, on September 23, one week after the landslide, they initiated construction work. Open-air barracks, a dispensary, a restaurant, a storehouse were built, and the work proceeded by mobilizing three hundred to five hundred laborers daily from Ulju-gun 20km away.

At this time, much of the heavy equipment accessible today was unavailable. Even if it had been, it would have been impossible to put the heavy equipment in because the mountain path was so narrow and steep. Therefore, Inescapably, along the 400m mountain path, stones, sod, pebbles, cement, tree seedlings, etc. were carried on people's back. Ones from special airborne troops were hired for the construction work at 70° gradient and over 100m length of slopes. After the engineering works were complete, *Lespedeza* and grass seeds were sown. Barley seeds were also scattered in secrecy.

On November 1, President Park revisited here accompanied by mayors and provincial governors from around the country. The visit was probably to demonstrate his principle of "five percent instruction, and ninety-five percent check". At President Park's request for natural-looking finishes, even in special methods of construction, the breast wall was finalized by attaching natural rocks. In April the next year, at the time of evaluation meeting with the president, the fact that the grass was completely green in the construction area was highly praised.

In reality, it was not grass but barley. The Ministry of Home Affairs has come to use this place as a demonstration site for educating mayors, county heads and Eup and Myeon heads around the country about erosion control. [1]

Photo 42. Pictures of gradual restoration after special erosion control at Ulju-gun in 1972 to protect the Ulsan industrial complex.

Erosion-Control Project for Yeongil District Admired by the World

Among President Park's achievements on reforestation of desolate land, the most widely known is the erosion-control project for Yeongil District, Gyeongbuk. It is well known because the project seemed impossible. On September 17, 1971, President Park specially visited this group of desolate lands while inspecting Saemaul at Munseong-ri, Gigye-myeon, Yeongil-gun. This is the place where an immense area totaling 4,500 ha over 115 villages was like a desert, without a single tree or blade of grass.

As a special district with soil composed of pelite and shale, the place had become a hot desert because weather erosion had broken down rocks and stones so that the topsoil washed away in rain and became hard when it was dry. Since the initiation of erosion-control projects in our country in 1907, there had been over fifty small-scale projects executed in this area, all without success.

Photo 43. Erosion-control work at Yeongil District was literally a bloody fight on 4,500 ha. All special techniques of public works had to be complemented by airborne troops.

After Korea-Japan relations became normalized in the mid 1960s, airlines began traveling from Tokyo to Seoul. This desert-like region was the first Korean territory these airlines passed through. As already noted, President Park, on his return to Korea after formally visiting West Germany in 1964, was brokenhearted to see this region. But in those days, all the people returning home after business trip overseas and even foreigners felt very sorry about it. Earth and sand running from this region had raised the riverbed of the Hyeongsan River and buried Yeongil-Bay area in piled up silt. It had also caused a tremendous hindrance to the construction of POSCO (Pohang Steel Company). In addition, this region had a history of failed erosion-control project executed under President Park's orders after the Forest Service became independent.

"This place is the gateway to an international airline. So keep working to recover the abandoned land by setting up a fundamental countermeasure." wrote President Park, issuing in 1971 an order to Gang Bong-Su, head of the Forest Service. Gang began by planning a trial project beginning in 1972 in an effort to develop a new method of construction. Research at the Forest Experiment Station on special erosion-control methods for this area indicated that it was most desirable to plant soil-improving alder and black locust trees as well as salt-and-wind-resistant black pine in holes 40cm deep and then add compost. However, the Forest Service did not conduct the restoration project itself.

In 1972, while passing through this place in a helicopter, President Park learned that no progress was being made in the erosion-control project after one year had passed. It seemed that when asked by the president, Gang failed to give a satisfactory answer. So after the start of the first Forest Rehabilitation project in 1973, President Park called on Sohn Soo-Ik, new head of the Forest Service, and gave a special order to reclaim the desolate land in Yeongil-district by any means possible. It was the first opportunity for Sohn, the new head, to exercise his capability.

First, Sohn asked that a helicopter landing field be created on the summit of the mountains so that the area could be monitored as often as possible. It was a move to enable mayors, county heads and relevant provincial officials to watch over the ongoing construction work from the summit of the mountain. The intent was to allow them to see the laborers work and to check on the site in person, as most erosion-control projects at the time tended to neglect toward the summit even when the job was accomplished well on the lower part of the mountain. It was Sohn himself who made the most frequent use of this helicopter field and who had directly received orders from the president.

Photo 44. Reward was in proportion to the difficult construction work. The picture shows before and after the erosion-control project.

Understanding that this region was made of special soils, Sohn decided to introduce a special method of construction, one executed in Ulju-gun the year before. Concrete was used around the hillside, and the slope was stabilized by driving the piles in. At places with a very steep slope, special laborers had to proceed by hanging from a climbing rope. It was the kind of life-risking construction work you could not possibly carry out without such a sense of mission. This region had many places with difficult construction details due to the rugged terrain. The laborers had much trouble, too. They had to carry stones and good earth from long distances on their backs.

Photo 45. In April 1975, in face of a strong rain storm, President Park visited the site of Yeongil District after driving on an unpaved road of 3 m width and encouraged the relevant officials. It is said that in the course of reporting, the briefing chart was blown away torn by the wind.

On April 17, 1975, President Park visited Odo-ri, Heunghae-eup, Yeongil-gun again. Because of rainy wind, the president rode not in a helicopter but in a jeep, which ran a snail's pace along an unpaved road just three meters wide. The path was so difficult that the president proposed to receive the report halfway up, but Park Sang-Hyun, Gyeongbuk Forest Bureau head, asked him to continue to the summit for a more detailed report and to encourage the officials and laborers at the site. At this sincere request, President Park willingly went up to the site. The company also included the Minister of Construction and the Presidential Chief of Staff.

After the inspection of the erosion-control site, President Park ordered workers to "install more drop works in the valley, dig a hole more deeply along the terraces, put good earth in, and plant a tree so that it might absolutely survive." He then granted an enclosure of money. Even after that, President Park inspected this place a couple of times to check on the progress and encourage early completion. Officials of the Forest Service and Gyeongbuk Provincial Office all agreed that the president's visits to the site and encouragement of the laborers even in such bad weather was the prime mover in leading the fierce battle in Yeongil District to a success. This place now stands as "a memorial of the presidential visit".

In 1977, after five years' work, the erosion control of 4,538 ha of desolate land at Yeongil District was complete at last. It was an enormous construction project involving 23.89 million seedlings, 101 tons of seeds, 4,161 tons of fertilizer, 22.41 million pieces of sod, 2.3 million blocks of stone, 2.1 million tons of fertile soil that was brought in, a total of 3.55 million workers and a budget of 3.8 billion won (US $7.85million).

Photo 46. Yeongil District erosion-control work was completed on 4,538 ha in five years that took the world by surprise. The picture shows the effect year by year.

The wonderful success of the erosion control project in Yeongil District, which had been considered hopeless, had an effect on the whole country. In 1977, there was a total 80,504 ha desolate land dispersed in fourteen districts around the country. However, after the success of the erosion-control project in Yeongil District, construction work continued in these places. Today they have been completely reforested, except for some regions that recently experienced forest fires. It reminds us of the phrase, "Like master, like man".

This Yeongil District, the site of the greatest battle in the history of

Korean erosion-control projects, has now been recognized as a twentieth-century miracle, winning praise from around the world. The story of the Yeongil District erosion-control project has been developed into a documentary movie with good reviews. To conserve this great history, the Gyeongbuk Province put up a "Yeongil Erosion-Control Completion Monument" at Yongcheon Village, Heunghae-eup. In 2007, officials established Erosion Control Memorial Park, equipped with halls of erosion-control history, education, and experiences, in 19 ha in the area of Odo Village, Heunghae-eup, Pohang City for public display.

There is a sequel too. Originally, effects of erosion-control project appeared gradually. The story of the erosion-control project at Yeongil District, almost forgotten even among forestry people after President Park's death, was first brought into relief in 1984 by Asahi Daily Shimbun's (Japan) report reading, "Korea's Desert Area at Yeongil Bay Disappeared". It must have been an interesting incident to Japanese reporters that the Yeongil District lying in ruins for a century or for over forty years after the end of Japanese Occupation had disappeared after all.

Phto 47. Grasses and trees are growing well during the first year of erosion-control work. It is because good soil was put in by digging a hole. This picture shows the desert-like soil in the background.

In the spring of 1984, 'Asahi Shimbun's reporter group visited Korea. Japanese reporters who had arrived at the site ushered by the Forest

Service combed out across the valleys, took pictures, and confirmed the site with precipices of dozens of meters high reforested. They didn't believe their eyes while reporting the method of construction stabilizing the slopes by using a tremendous amount of stones, putting concrete around the hillsides and driving piles in. They looked as if they were captivated by some magic. Then, they reported in detail and with color pictures the beautiful site of erosion control at the Yeongil District flooded with a series of green waves [1].

Chapter 10. Establishment of Large Complex of Chestnut Trees

Diverse Benefits of Forest

Trees give so many things to humans all without charge. It is natural that man may not comprehend the value. Basically, trees provide us with timber, pulp, and fuel. For every kind of animal, they provide a home. And there are more benefits. Let's count a few immediate things.

First, trees give us the function of purifying the air. Trees absorb carbon dioxide or other fumes emitted by man, factory, or vehicles, while producing oxygen. That's why humans are able to breathe. This is why planting a tree is encouraged even for a small piece of land among buildings.

Second, trees help to supply and store water. As briefly mentioned at the beginning of this book, mountain forests keep water in both leaf litter and the soil layer and run this water away bit by bit throughout the year. That's why the river keeps running even when there is no rain for a while, which enables man and other living beings to sustain their lives. The forest acts as a dam for man.

Third, trees provide beauty. When trying to survive, we do not take the time to look at a tree properly, but upon resolving the matter of food, clothing and shelter, we are more able to take interest in the beauty of a tree. That is why in a higher income country, decorative garden trees become more expensive. Even if you are not enjoying a high income, most people would say that they feel endorphin springing up at the sight of flowers blooming or tinted autumnal leaves on a tree.

Photo 48. A dam will be continuously supplied with water when surrounding mountains are fully stocked with trees.

Fourth, trees protect our environment. It is a tree that reduces damage from landslides or floods and that protects us from typhoons, thunder, or lightning. Each year we suffer from yellow dust because there are no trees to stop the dust arising in the desert of China.

Fifth, trees provide man with substitute food and essential nutrients. There are fruit trees like the apple, pear, peach, and persimmon trees, and nut trees such as the chestnut, jujube, walnut, and pine. These have nutrients that our common food crops or vegetables don't have, and in an emergency, they can even be a staple food. Despite the fact that these nut trees are so helpful to us, we didn't grow them properly as we did for apples and pears, just relying on the naturally occurring plants in the hills.

It is President Park who directed our attention to such nut trees for the sake of substitute provisions, a source of nutrition, and a source of farm village income, burning his desire to grow them. As he declared in the revolution pledge, we could tell how much he was a man who was racking his brains to find ways to help his starving brothers of the nation.

Photo 49. Among many diverse functions of dense forest, storing water in forests is extremely important to our people whose staple food is rice that requires much water for growth all the time.

The President's Love of the Chestnut Tree

President Park began to take a deep interest in nut trees in 1968 when he was pushing the Farmers' Income-Boosting Project. To encourage this project, the president sent out chestnut trees to many villages, while planting twenty chestnut trees in person in the tree-planting event of 1971 in Gwangju-gun, Gyeonggi-do, and emphasizing the substitute food effect of the trees. In 1972, he began to issue positive and strong orders to appropriate officials to cultivate the nut tree.

In 1972, it was eleven years after the military revolution, with the per capita national income rising to $319 from $78, and the Seoul-Busan Expressway had been completed. Additionally, it was one year before the completion of POSCO and the year of groundbreaking for subway line 1 in Seoul. In 1972, however, the farming people, who accounted for 40 percent of the whole population, still lived in thatch houses with smelly traditional restrooms, had to burn wood, and had no roads to carry coal briquettes on. The average income of three million farm houses failed to reach 80 percent of the urban households. Since the farming population failed to produce the people's food, it was inevitable to depend on a large amount of imports. A ruler would naturally have been troubled for increased food production and farmhouse income, trying to spread the fire of the Saemaul Movement just begun even more broadly.

It was at the New Year's tour of inspection in 1972 when President Park ordered the cultivation of nut trees. He particularly stressed the importance of planting chestnut trees. Here is part of his speech [6]

> "If we plant chestnut trees, chestnuts will be reaped in five years, which has a great profitability. They say 20 seom (2.88 tons) of chestnuts come out from 1 ha of land, an amount equal to the rice produced from the same area of a rice paddy. If we plant chestnuts for 100,000 ha and reckon one seom (144kg) of chestnuts for 40,000 won ($107), profits of around 80 billion won ($214million) will come in a year from mountains that have been wasted. ....That will make all village people work hard at a mountain, and the mountain will be made green spontaneously..........If the chestnut is mass-produced, by establishing a large-scale chestnut processing plant, it will be replaced with good-quality chestnut cake or substitute food, contributing greatly to self-sufficiency in food and, if necessary, it could be exported as well." [6]

Looking at the content, it is as if a teacher is explaining things in a new textbook to students. It reflects his possible worry that a simple order would not motivate the officials, who would be in the habit of responding, "It is difficult." or "It doesn't work well." The record has it that on March 24, 1972, while inspecting Saemaul site at Bangbae-dong, Seoul, he ordered related officials to "devise a plan for food by planting nut trees in the mountains around the country."

According to another record, in those days, there used to be the "Special Meeting for Economic Trends" managed by the Economic Planning Board. It was a monthly meeting in the presence of the president to report trends about the economy. At the end of every meeting, President Park always ordered that someone present a success case regarding the Saemaul project. Gang Bong-Soo, Head of the Forest Service, presented a report called "Success cases in the Efficient Use of Mountain Areas and a Measure for Reforestation by Nut Tree". Gang presented many cases from around the country and focused particularly on an apple orchards established in the mountain areas of Chungju, Chungbuk.

After the report, President Park simply said "Try to increase the income of farm villages." then left. Gang was greatly worried that his presentation had been insufficient because of the president's very simple response. However, it turned out to be a baseless anxiety. During the lunch with the economy-related cabinet members right after the presentation, President Park expressed a great interest in the multipurpose use of mountain areas. It was said that Gang was relieved when the president showed a deep interest in increasing the farmers' income through the use of mountain areas by asking, "Is it possible to cultivate apples in Chungju?" "How much income can we make by cultivating chestnut?" "Can it be profitable to cultivate paulownia in mountain areas?", and other such questions. [1] Apple production first started in Chungju area in 1907. However, President Park's interest activated research on apples in this area and Chungju apples became famous.

President Park ordered the planting nut trees as often as possible. The trees he designated in particular included the persimmon, chestnut, jujube, walnut, and pine, which even today become valuable and useful trees grown in the mountains. The records indicate that President Park had a particular interest in chestnut trees. It was probably because he believed that an active production of chestnuts would be helpful in solving problems in providing provisions. Kim Du-Yeong, ex-secretary of the Blue House, gave this testimony:

> "One day, President Park proposed dinner together after a day's work. After the meal, he saw a few short films together with the First Lady, Yook, which were documentaries such as "The Method of Cultivating the Chestnut" "Method of Cultivating Sweet Potatoes in Hotbed" "Policemen Defender of Dokdo" "People at Mining Station". President Park showed a big interest in chestnut trees, studying the method of cultivating them by taking notes." [27]

Photo 50. The picture shows how much President Park was interested in chestnut trees. He was so glad to reap five chestnuts two years after he himself planted the tree at the Blue House. He sent the nuts to the Minister of Home Affairs together with his sign (photo courtesy of Park Seung-Geol).

In the morning of April 5, 1971, President Park planted chestnut trees in an Arbor Day event in Gwangju-gun, Gyeonggi-do. In the afternoon, he planted another two-year-old chestnut tree in the yard of the Blue House for practicing cultivation in person. On September 25, 1973, President Park reaped five attractive chestnuts from this tree and, overjoyed, he informed Kim Hyun-Ok, Minister of Home Affairs, by letter that the tree had grown to a height of about 2.5 m and that it was possible to reap chestnuts from a four-year-old tree. He enveloped three chestnuts in his letter to Minister Kim, writing a detailed guide on how to give water and fertilizer. Minister Kim preserved the chestnuts in a bottle of alcohol and attached a copy of the president's memo, which the Minister had the related officials transcribe it.

There are about ten species of chestnut distributing around the world. These include four cultivated groups from Japan, China, Europe and America. The Korean chestnut tree, which belongs to the Japanese group, produces the largest chestnut (under 40 g, almost equal to a small egg) and provides a great help with food. Setting 1968 as the year for multipurpose development of forests, the Forest Service began to encourage the planting of chestnut trees on mountain hills as a means to develop a source of income.

President Park ordered an analysis and verification of the economic efficiency of the chestnut and encouraged farmers to plant it in great numbers. He issued a detailed order to plant chestnut trees on Arbor Day. His detailed order read, "In a valley near the village, plant Italian poplar or Hyun poplar. It is desirable to plant chestnut trees at the foot of a mountain and Korean white pines on a hillside".

In 1975, President Park established a new nut tree department in the Institute of Forest Genetics and increased the number of research personnel drastically, by thirty, to build the foundation for long-term research on the cultivation of nut trees. His action suggests how much he was devoted to securing food for the Korean people. In addition, some records indicate that the Economy Secretary's Office ordered research and development of Japanese-style chestnut cake and French-style hard-boiled chestnut cake. A July 1976 meeting, called "Monthly Meeting on Economic Trends" organized by the Economic Planning Board included a discussion on the processing of chestnuts. These records prove that President Park considered the cultivating of nut trees to be a national task, not just a Forest Service project. With food in short supply for the entire nation, what potential resources would he not have explored to deal with the matter of provisions?

Helped by President Park's special concern, the area planted with chestnuts in the southern part of the country continued to expand. In 1979, $14million worth of chestnuts were exported to Japan. Exports continued to increase and, in 1994, chestnuts worth $140 million were exported. Chestnuts became the number one exported produce item, winning the nickname of "filial tree". Globally, the total area of chestnut cultivation amounts to 343,000 ha as of 2007, while Korea's is 35,000 ha, about 10 percent of the global total. It is the world's third largest area, following those in China and Turkey.

Photo 51. A large-complex chestnut plantation was established on 100 ha in the mountain of Munsan-ri, Woidong-myeon Weolseong-gun, Gyeongbuk. President Park advised the planting of the chestnut positively because it would substitute for food and contribute to increasing the income of a farm village.

Chapter 11. Reforestation of the Country Using the Saemaul Movement

Farmers' Income-Boosting Project

Our people agree that the most successful policy after the establishment of the government itself is the Saemaul Movement. Of course, the Saemaul (new village in Korean) Movement is not a reforestation project. However, this movement included the forest-reclamation project in no small part. Two key concepts of the Saemaul Movement, self-reliance and cooperation, are the starting points of the fuel-wood forest establishment project in the 1960s. These concepts had been at the heart of the Forest Cooperative village units. This is why this book on the successful process of forest reclamation in this country cannot help addressing the Saemaul Movement. To understand the Saemaul Movement properly, we need to look at an earlier project called the "Farmers' Income-Boosting Project".

Although the Saemaul Movement started earnestly in early 1971, the Farmers' Income-Boosting Project started in 1968. In first announcing the project, President Park said the following:

> "To give the joy of life and reward to farmers who have been bound to solving the urgent need for food and clothing and knowing no pleasure in successive generations while living in thatch-roofed houses, this is my incessant wish. Until today, I have never spent a single day without remembering it. The Farmers' Income-Boosting Project's purpose is to help create a business that provides a large income for each locality in order to prepare the

basis for life filled with vitality for farmers and fisherman."

This thought by President Park can be paraphrased in a sentence, "The state is going to come forward to increase the income of farmers and fisherman."

Photo 52. A poor village farm in Daegu in March 1964, showing thatched houses and all bare hills at the back. President Park with sunglasses on is inspecting the reality of a farm village with low income.

The First Five-Year Economic Development Plan starting in 1962 the next year to the military revolution was successfully fulfilled in 1966. With an economic growth rate of 7.1 percent, no one would argue with called it "successful." However, farm villages still remained as they had been in the past. Though the government tried to increase income for farm villages by establishing policies that eliminated famers' high-interest debt, developing farming water, and redeveloping arable land, the cities' industrialization proceeded faster, increasing the gap in income between urban and rural communities.

In particular, farm villages could not escape the serious lack of food. Annually, April and May were the farm's hardship period, when food was running out and barley was still unripe. That is, the cruel reality called "spring poverty" held sway. A considerable part of the farming population subsisted literally on grass roots and tree bark. You may understand this condition by observing the North Korea's current rural residents, who often die of starvation .

One of those best aware of the tragic situation of the farm villages at that time was President Park. Despite some self-confidence in the country's economic development, he suffered bitter pain seeing the increasing gap in income between cities and farm villages. In his 1967 State of the Nation message, President Park clarified the fundamental frame of his agricultural policy. The agricultural and forestry policy should be based on a dramatic "agriculture and industry bilateral policy" and the farmers' income must be increased. The next year, the "Farmers' Income-Boosting Project" started. It established 1968 to 1971 as the four-year project period within the five-year economic development plan period ending in 1972. In 1968, the first year, it designated only forty-seven areas around the country. From the second year on, the plan expanded into ninety areas.

"The products" selected for the Farmers' Income-boosting Project included produce, livestock, and marine products. The project focused on items that could sold at a profit. The idea was to shift toward "commercial farming", that is, farming to make money, and away from just trying to subsist by growing rice, turnips, cabbage, potatoes, and sweet potatoes. There were a total of thirty-four items selected, including polyethylene greenhouse vegetables, hops, flax, sericulture, and laver.

Let's look into a couple of typical 'products' in more detail. First is the vegetable plots using polyethylene (vinyl) greenhouses. It was this time that the idea of making our menu green all year round was born. Until then, polyethylene greenhouse farming had not been prevalent in Korea. It makes sense because at that time polyethylene film was still relatively new and rare in Korea, and the necessary steel frames were in short supply. On the other hand, polyethylene greenhouses were becoming very popular in Japan. At a time when Korea still had numerous thatched-roof houses and illegally built shacks, in which electricity was available in only about 20 percent of farm villages, Japan's greenhouses were broad and high and had electricity on. In our country such a greenhouse would have looked like a house more brilliant than any farmhouses.

Photo 53. Scene of polyethylene greenhouse complex in Gimhae-gun, Gyeongnam. Growing vegetable plots is a typical example of the Farmers' Income-Boosting Project that started in 1968.

President Park decided to encourage polyethylene-greenhouse-grown vegetables as the most important product in the Farmers' Income-Boosting Project because Sunkyoung Chemicals Inc. (now the SK Group) had begun to produce polyethylene film in large quantities. Because there were not enough steel frames, however, the project started with "a low tunnel" method. Bamboo was split and both ends cut sharp and stuck in the levee of fields to form a frame, which was then covered with polyethylene film. Despite many difficulties, these greenhouses were a great success. Now, polyethylene broke the long-standing formula for farms, "the chief source of income for farmhouse equals rice" as, crops of greenhouses quickly took the place of rice.

Now, things have gone even further. Almost all produce comes from a greenhouse, including red peppers, lettuce, cucumbers, tomatoes, strawberries, and watermelons as well as every kind of mushroom, grape, tangerine, tara vine, and even poultry, such as hens and ducks. There is even a joke that all farming can be done in a polyethylene greenhouse except rice farming. So the year of 1968 was monumental turning points both for Korean farmers as suppliers and for city residents as consumers.

Ha Sa-Yong, who lived in Cheongwon-gun, Chungbuk Province, was a representative farmer who had succeeded with the Farmers' Income-boosting Project. After working as a farmhand for seven years, he purchased 660 m^2 of land with hard-earned money and started farming. Then, helped by the Farmers' Income-Boosting Project, he built a polyethylene greenhouse, grew vegetable plots, and made a large income. He was selected for the first place nationwide in a Farmers' Income-Boosting promotion contest and won the grand prize. He had an opportunity to make a presentation in person in the Monthly Meetings on Economic Trends in presence of the president in November 1969. Though it was a very unskilled presentation, his simplicity touched the president who, wiping his eyes, complimented him by saying, "That poor man has succeeded when he works hard. He really showed the spirit of I-can-do" and asked him to take a leading role in spreading greenhouse cultivation widely.

Photo 54. Ha Sa-Yong (front left) in Cheongwon-gun, Chungbuk became a successful farmer by making the most of the Farmers' Income-Boosting Project and gave a case presentation before the president (center) in November 1970. The president complimented him with tears coming into his eyes.

The second place winner in the Farmers' Income-Boosting Project must have been Fuji apple. At that time, Go Byeong-Woo, Director of Ministry of Agriculture and Forestry, and his company visited the Nagano Apple Institute in Japan.[26] At the entrance stood an apple tree bigger than a shade tree. Numerous apples were hanging from the branches. The guide explained that the number of apples was 1,800, but no two were the same breed. He said that as an experiment, all were grafted on using different cultivars. When Director Go Byeong-Woo flatly asked which apple cultivar was the largest and most delicious, the answer was the "Fuji apple". Perhaps because of the uniquely rash personality of a Korean, he decided on the spot and said "I will import the Fuji breed into Korea." and had them planted in an apple complex in Geochang District, Gyeongnam. That apple now stands as a representative apple of Korea, and is another brilliant success story of the Farmers' Income-boosting Project. [26)]

The third place can be referred to as the Jeju-do tangerine. Just before the outbreak of the Korean War in 1950, our people gathered donations and called Dr. Woo Jang-Chun, a world-famous Korea-born geneticist, from Japan. He attempted to improve our tangerines but failed to carry out the project because of the Korean War. Originally, the Jeju tangerine tree was as tall as the persimmon trees, and one had to pick the fruit by climbing a ladder. The price of tangerines was so high that there was a saying that two tangerine trees grown in the hedge could send one child to college. That is why it was also called the "college tree." Incidentally, Japan's tangerine was short, but it bore many fruits. Could that variety be the product that income-boosting project was looking for? The Farmers' Income Team then placed an order for 3,000 tangerine grafts from Japan's ministry of agriculture and forestry.

After testing the imported grafts in South Jeju county, the tangerine was spread free of charge across Jeju-do as part of the Farmers Income-Boosting Project. In addition, windbreaks around the orchards were also established free using Sugi trees. Today, forty years later, the traditional tall tangerine trees have disappeared, but the improved tangerine trees occupy every corner of Jeju-do. They supply fresh vitamins all year round at a price so low as to make one feel sorry for the producers. The Farmers' Income-Boosting Project surpassed its goal by the end of 1971. Its success was so profound that the household income of participating farmers and fishermen exceeded that of city workers. [26)] A secondary plan for the period from 1972 to 1976 was developed in cooperation with "Saemaul Income Increase Project."

The Saemaul Movement

In 1970, the opening the all sections of Seoul-Busan Expressway made the whole country reachable within a day. However, for rural communities, 80 percent still lived in thatched houses. Electricity reached only around 20 percent of them, and the remainder used small kerosene lamps. It was due to a power shortage caused by a sudden cut of the power supply from North Korea in May 1948. After that, South Korea suffered from an insufficient supply of electricity, with a generation capacity of only 870,000 kw in 1967. How humble that number is compared with the 78 million kw in 2012! Drinking water depended on one or two wells in a village, and if it was lacking, spring water had to be obtained for use. A house with a single cow was considered a rich one. At that time, the US magazine <*Life*> described the Korean farmer as "an animal that invariably carries an A-frame on his back and creeps along the levee of a rice paddy, as he has done for thousand years." The description gave a bad feeling, but it was a fact, too.

Photo 55. Shindo 1-ri, Cheongdo-eup, Cheongdo-gun, Gyeongbuk acted as a fuse to light the Saemaul Movement. President Park inspected this village that had been transformed into "Saemaul" even before the Saemaul Movement started.

When did President Park conceive of the idea of the Saemaul (or "New Village") Movement? Maybe it was right after the military revolution. The National Reconstruction Movement announcement on June 12, 1961, included a call for Koreans to "stand together in cooperation and with the spirit of self-reliance and self-help..... ", but it didn't refer to farm villages specifically. What remains as the first record of the movement is President Park's manuscript in his own handwriting for a speech made to the Ri and Dong Cooperative heads in August, 1962 the next year.

> "Of late, I have been to farm villages in the area of Honam. The movement in Jeonnam for establishing a model farm village is certainly "an evergreen tree movement", one that is igniting a revolution in our country's rural community. The purpose of this movement is, "Let's make a decent living"........ In such a village, there were sound and enthusiastic farm community leaders .... They say heaven helps those who help themselves. The government cannot help farmers without such a spirit of self-help......"

Photo 56. Slogan hanging on the front of the event indicates that the basic spirit of the Saemaul Movement is diligence, self-reliance and cooperation. Picture shows the Nationwide Saemaul Leaders Rally.

There was an opportunity for such an idea to be carried into action. In July 1969, the area of Gyeongnam and Gyeongbuk suffered great flood damage. On August 4, on his way to Busan by special train for inspecting these areas' flood damage repairs, President Park found a village in unusually good order near the railroad and stopped the train. It was the village of Shindo 1-ri, Cheongdo-eup, Cheongdo-gun, Gyeongbuk, which had been completely restored from flood damage. With its thick forest, its broadened inner path, its completely improved roofs, its tidily trimmed up fences, it had a living environment remarkably different from other villages. Answering the president, who was deeply impressed, they said that a resolution was made by the village residents in which they would build a more livable village by repairing and widening the roads and further cleaning the environment with voluntary cooperation.

The next year, on April 22, 1970, at the governors' meeting on drought damage, President Park introduced the case of Shindo village and advocated the "New Village Care Movement", appealing to the farmers' efforts for self-help. This was a historic day, and even now it is commemorated as the day for advocating the Saemaul Movement. He said,

> "Heaven helps those who help themselves. Without the voluntary will of residents, a village couldn't rise to its feet forever. If village people come forward with volition, they are able to rise in a couple of years if the government offers small help. Leaders of a village should gather together, devise plans, and conduct research. It is our officials' responsibility to make an atmosphere so that village people may decide something they must do and other things to receive help from the government. Will this village be able to develop when you have to carry a burden on your back from four km away because there is no road for a car to get into the village? This year we should improve a road and build a bridge. If it is above the residents' ability, the county or province will help. This movement could be called "New Village Care Movement."

This quotation contains the basic spirit of the Saemaul Movement, conveying his vague idea that has since become more concrete. There was a certain difference in this plan. Whereas the Farmers' Income Boosting Project was simply for raising the farmers' income, the Saemaul Movement would deal with the general development of farm villages.

In accordance with this instruction, the Ministry of Home Affairs instructed the heads of Eup and Myeon on the New Village Care

Movement for four days beginning October 5, 1970. On March 24, 1971, President Park advocated the "Sweep the Front of My House Movement" and performed street cleaning together with the Blue House staff. President Park selected the official name of the "Saemaul Movement", and established a department exclusively responsible for the movement in the Ministry of Home Affairs on August 19, 1971. On September 29, he defined the spirit of the Saemaul Movement as "diligence, self-reliance and cooperation."

On March 7, 1972, Saemaul Undong Center regulations were enacted by the presidential order to start the Saemaul Movement officially. President Park told the governors' meeting that the core projects of that year would be the Saemaul Movement and nationalization of the Saemaul spirit. Then, President Park showed such enthusiasm that he created music and verse for a Saemaul song himself on April 21.

Photo 57. In 1972, women in Cheongdo-gun, Gyeongbuk, are carrying blocks made of cement supplied by the government. It is considered that women contributed no less than men in the Saemaul Movement.

The wheel of history gets power from an unexpected place. During a meeting on the New Village Care Movement on October 5, 1970, Kim Seong-Gon of the Republican Party proposed a special loan for the cement industry in response to a severe financial difficulty due to excess production. Unexpectedly, President Park told Kim Chung Yum, Presidential Chief of Staff, "Seek a plan to transfer the excess cement to the New Village Care Movement."

In October 1970, 300 to 350 sacks of cement were supplied to 34,665 villages around the country. The precondition was that the cement must be used for the villages' joint work. Examples provided included expanding a village's path, constructing a small bridge, improving a well facility, establishing a public bath, rebuilding a small stream bank, and making a communal wash place. The final decision, however, was totally and autonomously entrusted to village people. The results of the free cement supply varied from village to village. President Park ordered a post project evaluation, which revealed that only 16,600 villages out of 34,665 made good use of the cement.

In 1972, the second year of the movement, President Park ordered that the supply of five hundred sacks of cement and one ton reinforcing steel rod be provided only to the 16,600 villages that had good results in the previous year. The Ministry of Home Affairs was embarrassed by this order. Likewise, the ruling Republican Party was alarmed and opposed the plan strongly, arguing that the excluded villages wouldn't vote for the Republicans at the next election. However, President Park kept to his principle of supporting villages that helped themselves by exercising the spirit of self-reliance. Similarly in the farm electrification project, the president ordered that villages with good results from the Saemaul Movement should receive power first, regardless of the distance from the electric pole, and that villages should not receive power merely in the order of nearness to the power source.

In the third year, too, President Park, on the basis of the enthusiasm of the residents, divided 35,000 villages around the country into three grades and excluded those in the lowest grades. It was an effort to reward good conduct. Incidentally, a wonderful response occurred among the indolent and neglectful farmers. The movement became an opportunity to inspire competitive and cooperative minds in the villages excluded from support. At last, the Saemaul Movement spread out like wildfire across the whole nation. [10]

The Saemaul Movement was a great success. Kim Chung Yum, Chief of Staff in the Blue House described a few factors behind the success. [9] President Park started the Saemaul Movement for environmental improvement of farm villages but connected it to increasing income, which was more urgent. The first case was the supply of "Unification Rice" developed by Professor Heo Mun-Hoi of Seoul National University.

It was planted widely starting in 1972. As a result, the Unification Rice cultivar produced 437 kg rice per 1,000 m^2, while the output of conventional rice cultivars averaged 329 kg, a 33 percent increase in production. The thirty-three percent increase in production by a new breed was a radical revolution almost unheard of globally, even surpassing the productivity of Japan, which ranked first in the world at the time. That is, the Saemaul Movement accomplished the great task for self-sufficiency of rice, our staple food, and helped end starvation in farm villages; a stubborn problem for 5,000 years of Korean history.

Photo 58. The Saemaul factory in a farm village provided many jobs for youths in rural communities, directly contributing to increasing the income of the farming population.

The second case was the Saemaul Movement's connection to the Second Five-Year Farmers' Income-Boosting Project (1972-1976), through which greenhouse vegetable cultivation, beekeeping, button mushrooms, fruits, tobacco, aquaculture, beef cattle were encouraged. An additional step in the movement to improve non-farming income was to invite a Saemaul factory into a farm village. This increased per capita farmhouse income from $137 in 1970 to $300 in 1975 and to around $700 in 1978, more than a five-fold increase in eight years. The income difference between urban and rural communities decreased. Thus in 1967 a farmer's income stood at 60 percent of the city worker's, but after 1974 the farmer's income began to surpass the city worker's.

Another project that contributed to raising the farm villages' income and cooperative spirit was the First Ten-Year Forest Rehabilitation Plan, which started in 1973. Sohn Soo-Ik, a newly appointed Forest Service Head, greatly expanded the village tree nursery using Saemaul organization, through which it was possible to raise the common income of a village.

The Saemaul Movement that started in rural communities gradually spread to factories and cities. Factory or city workers were mostly from farm villages. Impressed by the farmers' change in mental attitude as well as the appearance of their farm villages, they had the idea to spread the Saemaul Movement into their workplaces. In line with this, President Park ordered the relevant government departments to create City Saemaul, Factory Saemaul, and School Saemaul Movements. The factory Saemaul project focused on developing labor-management harmony, and raising productivity. The City Saemaul project emphasized clean residential environments, keeping order, being nice to neighbors, and respecting one's parents and the elderly, and afterward even a movement toward the conservation of nature. [9]

Elimination of Political Purposes from Saemaul Movement

The Saemaul Movement is considered to have been a training ground for Korea's democracy. In its initial stage, village joint projects included projects to open the village driveway and to broaden its inner path, but for this land the government didn't pay compensation. Instead, owners of the land on both sides of the road had to donate part of his farmland to the village, while other residents had to provide the labor. All of this took place autonomously, and proceeded after democratic discussion and agreement.

In addition, the Saemaul women's association was organized to take charge of one part of the Saemaul Movement. This involvement drastically improved the status and voices of women in farm villages. In particular, housewives were engaged in a campaign to eradicate men's drinking and gambling, and they took the lead in saving. A good testimony of this effort was that saving deposits in the Agricultural Cooperative Bank amounted to just $12 per household in 1971, but they increased to $507 in 1978. [9]

From the start, President Park thoroughly excluded political agendas from the Saemaul project. At the beginning of the 1970s, the Republican Party proposed the idea that the Saemaul leader in each village be signed up as a party member. However, President Park said, sour-faced, "No one should use the Saemaul Movement politically. The Saemaul Movement should be sublimated to a pure popular movement intended to make farm populations, villages and the state better–off by arousing the spirit of diligence, self-reliance, and cooperation among farmers." Now it is logical that if the Saemaul Movement had been used for political purposes, it would never have succeeded and advanced into a development model for developing countries, as it is today.

Some would suspect that the Saemaul Movement may have had political purpose because it was followed by enacting of the Yushin Constitution. In fact, for over a decade, President Park always asked that two cases of successful Saemaul Movement projects be presented during each Monthly Special Meeting for Economic Trend. These presentations, given by the farmers themselves in front of the government ministers, were the last parts of meetings. Could the custom of hearing these presentations have lasted for a decade if the Saemaul Movement had been only a political show? [10] Under the Yushin system, the presidential election was in fact perfunctory. Therefore, there was no need to mobilize any organization for the election in order to maintain the regime. This must have been the reason President Park could have led the Saemaul Movement purely and for the long-term.

The Saemaul Movement in the 1970s totally transformed the picture of the Korean farm villages. First, because all villages had a road open to automobiles, community bus routes formed, and the use of motorcycles spread. Second, electricity was supplied everywhere around the country. In 1970, electrification reached just 27 percent of farmhouses. By 1979, electricity was installed in 99 percent or 2.78 million households. Thatched roofs were replaced with tile or slate. In addition, simple water service was installed to all farmhouses, and in an area where it was difficult to install, a water pump was installed on the existing well to let water into the kitchen. By 1978, telephone lines connected all villages, and stream banks were repaired. Also, a village hall was set up in each village to be used as a conference room, joint purchase room or day-care center.

Photo 59. President Park, after listening to a woman worker, opened the way to continuing education of young workers by establishing company-attached evening school.-

One anecdote that reveals President Park's inmost heart about the Saemaul Movement was told by Kim Seong-Jin, former Minister of Culture and Information. [17] One day, President Park inspected a factory that produced exports. Watching young technicians from a farm village working diligently, he asked a girl technician what was her wish. "I want to learn English. Not knowing English, I cannot understand clearly the English words supervisor says" At this unexpected response, tears came into President Park's eyes probably because he remembered his poor childhood. He asked the company president standing at his side, "Can't there be a way for these youths to learn subjects?" The company president agreed that he would set up a Saemaul evening school.

Sometime later, an evening school corresponding to a middle school opened. Technicians graduated despite the difficulty of working by day and studying by night. But the Ministry of Education refused to confer a middle school diploma. Probably because the class performance fell short of the regulation. Learning this, President Park was furious. He issued an immediate order to tear apart and mend such a regulation. Finally, graduation from middle school was approved, and the Saemaul middle schools were set up in various locations.

Kim Seong-Jin assesses the factory Saemaul Movement as follows:

"An enterprise that was devoted to the factory Saemaul Movement exchanged management information and discussed difficulties through a monthly, joint labor-management conference, which solidified mutual trust and formed a labor-management community. Among slogans created by the Factory Saemaul Movement headquarters was "As workers consider factory work mine, so managers consider workers his family". From the atmosphere of today's industrial society, this movement is considered most necessary. (Kim Seong-Jin, <*Factory Saemaul Movement and Saemaul School*>

There is another story that provides a glimpse into President Park's mind on the Saemaul Movement. Professor Ryu Tae-Yeong of Konkuk University had given advice to the government on early development of the Saemaul spirit. He recollected as follow: [25]

"By the special order from the president, I gave a lecture on the Saemaul Movement for three hours for about 250 persons including the Blue House's special aides, senior secretaries, administrators, presidential security officers. I stressed my argument passionately, comparing cases from Denmark and Israel with the reality of Korea's farm village. After the lecture, I was invited by the first lady to a family dinner and had a single conversation with the president and first lady until past 11 pm. The president, forgetting about tiredness, was seriously concerned about the country's development and farming population, how to make our peasants get out of poverty, asking endlessly about cases of advanced countries. For the first time in my life, I was able to know his humanity, and his tenacity of purpose as a national leader. I felt that his biggest worry was over national development, the improvement of backward farm village life, and farmers' welfare, racking his brains to find solutions to them." [25)]

Photo 60. Farm villages turned into a rich district owing to the Saemaul Movement, such as roof improvement, pavement of roads, etc.

Since 1974, farmhouse income increased to the point of surpassing city workers'. In April 1980, corresponding to the tenth anniversary of the Saemaul Movement, there were 35,950 village halls, 44,000 km of newly constructed roads, 40,000 km of broadened village roads, and 4,440 km of new water channels. The 1.4 million won ($2,892, based on exchange rate of 484 won per dollar) annual farmhouse income goal had been set for 1981, but was reached in 1977.

Jo Gap-Je, former *Chosun Ilbo* executive editor, also commented on the historic meaning of the Saemaul Movement:

"This was the first time ever in our history that farmers participated in creating history voluntarily and with initiative, shedding passive awareness of the subjects. In addition, by allowing residents themselves to decide on the content of the

Saemaul projects through discussion, it became an opportunity to sprout out 'grass roots democracy'." [4)]

Park Jin-Hwan, former special presidential aid for the economy, played a leading role in creating the Saemaul Movement. He explained the importance of cooperation in this movement:

"Generally, in cooperation one plus one is two (1+1=2). However, man's power makes one plus one is alpha (1+1= α). This alpha can be zero (0) or, if combined between two who are congenial to each other, alpha can be as large as infinity. On the other hand, grouping people not made for each other only causes disagreement, and alpha can be a minus. A cooperative spirit in the Saemaul Movement is a movement toward making this alpha build up to infinity." [10)]

Saemaul Movement and Forest Reclamation

The Saemaul Movement had been inseparably related to the forest-reclamation project. In December 1961, the military government enacted the Forest Law for the first time, and made each Village Forestry Cooperative turn a forest project, such as the establishment of a fuel-wood forest, into village cooperative business. It was a legal institution to make sure that one failing to participate was not allowed to gather fuel wood. In 1973, as a part of the ten-year forest rehabilitation project, the village nursery was a representative business operating through cooperation among residents. The cooperative business resulted from the forest project. It was thus through the Forest Cooperative that a spirit of cooperation among residents toward the common village interest was cultured, and "cooperation" which later became the basic spirit of the Saemaul Movement, was naturally advanced through such experience.

The Saemaul Movement also included improvements of farm village furnaces. A traditional furnace, with its large opening, consumed much fuel and lost much heat. Kim Hyun-Ok, Minister of Home Affairs, ordered research on improving furnaces believing that a village's saving of fuel wood was a precondition for forest reclamation. Additionally, the "Rid My Village of a Red Land Campaign" was in progress. This campaign had the purpose of planting trees on a small piece of land and hills with bare ground in red color, which became a model case for village people, not led by government, to volunteer in planting trees.

The government decided to attract a Saemaul factory to a farm village in order to connect the Saemaul Movement to the farm village income, and this rendered help in the forest reclamation effort. Gathering fuel wood, or raking up fallen leaves and branches from a mountain, was a laborious job, taking much time. Farmers with a higher income through the Saemaul factory, however, were ready and able to purchase convenient 19-holed coal briquettes instead. Through the Saemaul Movement, which had broadened and paved village roads, the transport of 19-hole briquettes to remote villages was now possible. This substitute fuel decreased the need to gather fallen leaves, which in turn made the forest soil more fertile and achieved forest protection and restoration naturally. In sum, the forest-reclamation project engendered a cooperative spirit that gave rise to the Saemaul Movement, which in turn helped forest reclamation by spreading the use of coal briquettes.

Photo 61. One of the basic spirits of the Saemaul Movement was cooperation. Initially, the spirit of cooperation started with the project of nursing young trees.

On April 22, 2010, marking the fortieth anniversary of the Saemaul Movement's beginning, *Chosun Ilbo* daily news conducted a poll of 1,500 adults around the country. The largest number of respondents (59.1 %) selected the Saemaul Movement as the policy that had the biggest effect on national development since the establishment of the government in 1948. To another question about when our country's economy had developed dramatically, more respondents (33.8 %) picked the 1970s when Saemaul Movement started than any other period. Nearly all of the respondents (95.8 %) estimated that the Saemaul Movement had contributed to national development.

The Saemaul Movement has now spread to 130 countries of the world. China, the largest agricultural country, with a population of 0.9 billion farmers, recommended the "New farm village Movement", which was literally put into Chinese from Saemaul Movement, as part of "Eleventh Five-Year Economic Development Plan" (2006-2010). This was a policy established after research on the Saemaul Movement in which China sent leading members of the Chinese Communist Party Central Policy Research Team to Korea in 2005. In July 2009, US President Obama visited Kenya, his father's home country, and said, "To escape from poverty, you should make Korea's Saemaul Movement an example."

The Saemaul Movement may be analogous with the current phenomenon known as "Hallyu". It has been spread abroad since 1972, and 4,974 persons from 109 countries, as of 2012, have been enrolled in the regular courses of Saemaul education, and 54,927 persons have visited Saemaul Movement Center. The Saemaul Movement Center joined DPI (United Nations Department of Public Information) as a member and is taking the initiative in spreading it. [2]

"Saemaul Movement" appears in the *Encyclopedia Britannica* (UK) as a noun. In 1996, the Saemaul Movement was presented in France as a topic on a college entrance exam essay. It is certain that the Saemaul Movement is one of Korea's representative brands. [2]

Part 4.

Period of Forest Service under the Ministry of Home Affairs

Chapter 12. Transfer of the Forest Service

Complaint about the Forest Service

The year 1972 marked the twelfth year since President Park had come into power. During the previous eleven years, President Park had many accomplishments in the area of economic development and forest reclamation. He exceeded the quotas of the first and second five-year economic development plans earlier than expected, enacted the Forest Law right after the revolution, and swept away illegal timber cutters, citing illegal cutting as one of the five major social ills in Korea. To solve the need for firewood for farm villages, he ordered the planting of hundreds of millions of fuel-wood trees by setting up a five-year fuel-wood forest establishment plan in 1968, planting tens of millions of Italian poplars all over the country, and ordering that railroad ties and telegraph poles be made from cement.

Furthermore, he separated the Forest Service from the Ministry of Agriculture and Forestry, and expanded its organization, designated greenbelts and national parks, and helped to introduce or breed superior trees. Tree planting mobilized nearly all the people, from little children to public servants with diverse motives, including commemoration of soldiers being sent to Vietnam. However, the reforestation project is totally different from erecting buildings. In architecture, ordinarily a large building will be completed in three or four years, presenting its magnificent appearance. Trees are different. If a hundred trees are planted and committed to nature, would half of them grow properly and reach their full height? Even if they do grow to have a magnificent appearance, it can take several decades.

The strong will of President Park on reforestation must have been attributed to his self-confidence. "I-can-do" spirit was his faith. As he reached his twelfth year in power, however, it seemed President Park had some skepticism. Still, there were ugly, bare mountains everywhere, and officials didn't always follow the instructions.

On August 19 and 20, 1972, for just two days, heavy rain fell in the Seoul, Gyeonggi, Gangwon, and Chungbuk areas. A total of 314 mm poured down in Suwon, which resulted in great flood damage in the Anyang-Shiheung area. There were 301 people dead or missing. This flood damage was the heaviest ever during President's Park's eleven years of service as president. Since he had been unusually devoted to the conservation of rivers and forests, how heartbreaking it must have been when he visited the site of flood damage?

Besides, the forest-reclamation project is not just for the prevention of flood. Korea is still a country focused on rice farming. Producing 1 kg of rice takes a few thousand liters of water, and this tremendous amount of water supply is quite impossible without dense forests. This was why Korea's bare mountains determined a good or bad harvest of rice, depending on the precipitation patterns the same year. What could President Park have thought facing this heavy flood damage?

It seemed that President Park was considerably dissatisfied with the Forest Service. First, Kim Yeong-Jin, assigned as the first Forest Service Head in 1967, set up 35-year plan for forest reclamation at the end of 1968. It was a large-complex reforestation plan focused on timber production in remote areas. It also required a long period. It was a plan quite alien to the more immediate realities of the need for fuel-wood forests and of danger of landslides at any moment. The president's idea was to reforest the bare mountains as early as possible.

Second, in 1971, the president issued a very earnest order to Gang Bong-Su, the second Head of the Forest Service, about the erosion-control project at Yeongil District, Gyeongbuk (See Part 3, 'Battle in Yeongil District'). However, the Forest Service established a plan to start the erosion control work in 1973 after a thorough experiment in 1972 to find the best way of erosion control for the Yeongil district's unique soil. Riding a helicopter and learning that no progress had been made on the site in 1972, President Park issued the same order again, which caused significant upheaval in the Forest Service. The failure must have given the president the feeling that neither the Forest Service nor its head properly grasped the importance and urgency of the presidential order.

It seemed that President Park was not happy with himself either. He started to review the system. On January 12, 1973, the president held a new-year's press conference marking the first year of Yushin. His statement reads:

> "........To make efficient use of the country, we should facilitate developing the four major river basins as well as other major rivers, ... and establish ten-year plan to make the mountains completely green. That will be the way to make our country a beautiful place for us to live in........"

In this statement, it may not seem so interesting that he briefly mentioned the ten-year plan for forest reclamation. It was important, however, that the president had never consulted this matter with the Forest Service in advance. After the press conference, Kim Yeon-Pyo, Reforestation Section chief of the Forest Service, inquired of the presidential secretariat because no one was aware of the president's concerns ahead of time.

Forest Service Transferred to Ministry of Home Affairs

With this much discontent about the Forest Service, President Park appointed Sohn Soo-Ik as the third Forest Service Head on January 15. The naming of a third head in six years was an unusually frequent change in President Park's personnel practice.

Then, several interesting things happened in succession. On January 22, in a presidential inspection of the Ministry of Home Affairs, President Park voiced his complaints about the Forest Service. How odd it was that the president, who couldn't be ignorant of the Forest Service's being under the Ministry of Agriculture and Forestry, visited the unrelated Ministry of Home Affairs for his complaints about the Forest Service. Officials of the Home Affairs were in blank amazement, but they had to diligently note down what the president said because anything given to officials by the president was an overriding necessity. The president went on seriously: [29]

> "First, measures of forestry that have been makeshift and mediocre working procedures should be basically reviewed in this phase. We couldn't apportion a large budget to the Forest Service. But if even within that scope, had they used it effectively, the mountains would have been much greener and the trees been much taller............ Second, this year, we should punish heavily any act of raking up leaf litter even by making a law when necessary. For fuel wood, we may allow harvesting grass or cutting off branches out of the fuel-wood forest, but never allow farmers to rake up leaf litter. ...." [29]

Photo 62. Letters of the "Ministry of Home Affairs" put up on the mountainside – small but vivid. Reforestation project mobilizing the administrative power of the Ministry of Home Affairs went on much more intensively than the age of the Forest Service under the Ministry of Agriculture and Forestry, leading to an amazing result after all.

For several days thereafter, it seems there was no action from President Park. Among officials of the Ministry of Home Affairs, there must have been idea that "censure about the Forest Service" was just a passing thought on the part of the president. However, other events were going on at another place.

The happening was testified in detail by Sohn Soo-Ik, then Head of Forest Service.[11] This was February 13, not less than a month since Sohn proceeded to his post:

> "In the president's move to the Chungnam Provincial Office after finishing his annual inspection of Chungbuk, an urgent instruction was delivered that the Forest Service Head participate in the next meeting. When (by helicopter) I arrived in the middle of the meeting, the president even checked by asking, 'Is the Forest Service head present?' But even after finishing the provincial meeting, he didn't mention anything to me, so I was completely at a loss as to what to do.
>
> The president's company started on their way back to Seoul. So I was just starting to run on the highway with the presidential attendants. Then, the president's car pulled over, and the secretary ran up to me and asked me to get in the president's car. In the car, Kim Hyun-Ok, Minister of Home Affairs, had been in company. For a considerable time, the president kept silent but then said to me, "Have you got acquainted with your job yet?" "How is the ten-year plan going?" and then suddenly uttered, "What do you think about transferring the Forest Service to the Ministry of Home Affairs?"
>
> Without time to study the pleasure of Minister Kim Hyun-Ok, I answered carefully, "It is up to the ruler's decision, you know, because the government's agency organizations are a means of reign. Forest may have a good point being in the Ministry of Agriculture and Forestry, which belongs to the same primary industry. But in view of the urgency and absolute need for forest reclamation, it would also be advantageous to go to the Ministry of Home Affairs, which has local administration and police force in charge."
>
> At this time, President Park issued three orders to me in the car. Talk to the prime minister tomorrow and proceed with moving the Forest Service to the Ministry of Home Affairs. Proceed with reforestation intensively since Minister Kim will come forward actively. Fulfill the job of forest reclamation by consultation with

Minister Kim. The president then asked, "What can I do to help you fulfill the forest reclamation at an early stage?"

To his question I answered this way: It would be good to establish forest subsections at Eups and Myeons around the country, putting staff in exclusive charge of forests but it would take an increase of personnel of over 5,000 people. So what about newly appointing heads of Forest Bureaus for each province as confidants to each provincial governor, and forest section heads for cities and counties as confidants to mayor and county head? Finally, the president accepted this, opening the way for many promotions of forestry officials, their participation in local governors' advisors meeting, and an opportunity for the forestry position to be promoted to mayor and county head. When I reported it the next day to the Prime Minister Kim Jong-Pil, he even added annotation saying, "Now I got it! That's why he attached the well-achieving Gyeonggi governor to the Forest Service Head!" It was because sending out a provincial governor to the Forest Service Head was then perceived as a demotion rather than a promotion.

Photo 63. Sohn Soo-Ik, Head of the Forest Service, assisted President Park's will toward forest reclamation perfectly in his six years of incumbency with his careful planning capability, frequent visits to the fields and meticulous checks as the field commander.

After such vicissitudes, by passage of the National Government Organization Act at an emergency cabinet meeting on February 23, 1973 and promulgation on March 3, the Forest Service was transferred to the Ministry of Home Affairs six years after its launch. In 1967, President Park allowed the Forest Bureau under the Ministry of

Agriculture and Forestry to be independent as the Forest Service. However, the Minister of Agriculture and Forestry couldn't afford to pay attention to the Forest Service's forest-reclamation project because he had a more urgent task in solving food problems. Additionally, the projects of land clearing or establishment of grass fields often conflicted with the forest-reclamation project. This was why the Forest Service failed to strongly carry out forest-reclamation project under the Ministry of Agriculture and Forestry.

In most countries, the Forest Service naturally belongs to the Ministry of Agriculture and Forestry. So why did President Park take such a strong action? The transfer of Forest Service to Ministry of Home Affair in charge of the Saemaul Movement, local administration, and the police strengthened forest protection using both local government and police organization. This established a triad system of provincial governor, mayor, and county head for tree planting and general management of the forests, a police chief for protective control, and forestry officials for technical guidance.

Kim Hyun-Ok and Sohn Soo-Ik

We have seen several times how firm President Park's will toward forest reclamation was. But when he even changed the affiliation of the Forest Service, it was not simply will but rather obsession toward forest reclamation. President Park went for victory by reorganization of the system. So who are Kim Hyun-Ok and Sohn Soo-Ik, so entrusted by President Park as his hand and foot? We need to know about them.

Kim Hyun-Ok was selected by President Park and as mayor of Seoul when he was till mayor of Busan. He then became the minister of Home Affairs. Indeed, he was on a fast track, but actually it was the result of his capability rather than good fortune. When he was the Seoul mayor, he pushed for an epoch-making urban planning, and development of the Yeouido and Gangnam areas, which had been a constantly flooded area, with drastic expansion of roads and a focus on flood control of the Han River. He is also the figure who established the current framework of the Seoul city by attempting the construction of apartment houses for the first time.

Kim Hyun-Ok astutely knew what his duties were and what the person who appointed him wanted from him. In addition, he combined his unique leadership with a passionate work initiative and his excellent grip on the organization.[31] Kim Hyun-Ok is famous for his thorough aid to the president as he took charge of the Ministry of Home Affairs in October 1971. Understanding the president's mind, he selected the Saemaul project and forest-reclamation project as two of the major national policy tasks of the Ministry of Home Affairs and proceeded to carry out his duties. His great concern with forest reclamation, rigorous orders, and full support of the Forest Service will be described further later.

Sohn Soo-Ik, third Forest Service Head, graduated from Law School at Seoul National University. He worked in the Blue House as a secretary for political affairs and gained the confidence of the president. Joining the Ministry of Home Affairs as head of Local Bureau, he participated in originating the Saemaul Movement, and finished the national roadside remodeling project between Seoul and Chuncheon within a year. This work inspired a compliment from the president. Later, this project was designated as a demonstration area of successful street remodeling.

Sohn Soo-Ik then worked as Gyeonggi-do governor until the president directed him to perform a new mission as the Forest Service Head. Anyone could presume how he must have been dispirited to receive the announcement of appointment as Forest Service Head. Isn't promotion the highest value in a bureaucratic society? Thereafter, however, for six years he rewrote the history of forest reclamation for our country and the world, with responsibility and authority equivalent to a minister.

Sohn's activity as Forest Service Head will be detailed more fully later. But worth noting here is why President Park entrusted the forest-reclamation project to these two people, how these two people drove forward with their assignment, and the final result. By noticing them, you can understand President Park's ways of using his men and the key to his capability in accomplishing the most challenging goals.

Chapter 13. Full-Scale Forest Rehabilitation Project

Heavy Chemical Industry and Forest Rehabilitation at the Same Time

The era of the Forest Service under the Ministry of Home Affairs began on March 3, 1973. In the previous chapter, President Park's positive method of forest reclamation was characterized as "strong action." At that time, however, a "super-strong action" not comparable with other kinds was in preparation. It was not, however, directly related to forest reclamation. It was a constitutional crisis. On October 17, 1972 President Park dissolved the National Assembly, interrupting parliamentary activities, and promulgated the Yushin Constitution two months later, opening the way for a Korean president to serve for life.

These events are not mentioned in order to address the related politics, but rather to point out what changed in the forest reclamation project. In the past, there had been many cases where budget authorities raised questions when the president issued some instructions about forest reclamation. Or it could be that he was faced with negative cooperation from related agencies and local governments. Now, however, such "disloyalty" clearly died away, probably because of the powerful Yushin Constitution or Emergency Cabinet Meeting.

The 1973 saw the beginning of a great change in the history of our

Korean Peninsula. Construction of Korea's heavy chemical industry and the full-scale forest-reclamation project took off simultaneously. It was a great change tantamount to the Saemaul Movement, launched one year before, and the interruption of the constitutional government, which stupefied the entire country. On the side of the national economy, it was certainly a grave matter that could shake the whole country.

First, the author wants to introduce the speech about the launch of the heavy chemical industry by O Won-Chul, second senior secretary of the economy, who then stood at the core of planning. [18]

> On May 30, 1972 after the finish of the Export Expansion Meeting at the Capitol Building Hall, President Park called me out to the Blue House and said, "Tell me what industry we could rear to export ten billion dollars." I was alarmed because it was just eighteen months before that we attained a one-billion dollar target of exports, and until February this year, we had set the target amount of annual exports of five billion dollars by 1980. I proposed for the first time the content I had usually kept only as an idea in my mind.
>
> I told the President that the answer was the heavy chemical industry. In the case of Japan, it had focused on exporting light industry articles as the first step to reconstruct the economy that had fallen into ruins after the Second World War. It was just like our country now. Then, when attaining two billion dollar exports in 1957, the country immediately started building heavy chemical industry. By 1967, ten years later, it had achieved ten billion dollars in exports. Nowadays, mechanical and steel products are the main products of Japan.
>
> President Park immediately ordered the cabinet to establish a heavy chemical industry task force. While preparing for a South-North Korea meeting, President Park arranged for planning on the construction of a defense industry, ten billion dollar exports, and a heavy chemical industry at the same time. I think it was to achieve these goals successfully that he established a strong ruling system through the measure of the Yushin Constitution on October 17 of the same year. It seems that through Yushin, he wanted to organize national power and maximize efficiency.[18]

Dr. O Won-Chul and President Park must have believed that it was possible to proceed with these three goals simultaneously by integrating them into one system.[5] Their confidence at that time must have been great. They were about to hold a ceremony to mark the completion of the first stage of construction at the Pohang Iron & Steel Co., which three years earlier had been regarded with a dim view by many countries including the United States, because it had not been a business suited for Korea's immediate circumstances.

Photo 64. Constructing dockyard proposed by the president was unanimously opposed by all relevant officials. However, we have built up as the number-one shipbuilding country of the world at the turn of the twenty-first century.

On December 28, soon after the proclamation of the Yushin Constitution, the Ministry of Commerce announced a plan for achieving $10 billion annual exports by 1980 at the Export Expansion Meeting. Within several months, the target amount of exports doubled. President Park urged that: "the value of October Yushin depends on whether $10 billion of exports is achieved within the period. Go all out by focusing all policies of the government on the $10 billion target of exports."[5]

On January 31 the next year, President Park approved the "Report on Reorganization of Defense Industry and Industrial Structure" made by O Won-Chul, Chief Secretary, after four-hour discussion with Premier Kim

Jong-Pil, Finance Minister Nam Deok-Woo, Science & Technology Minister Choi Hyeong-Seop, as well as the National Defense, and Commerce and Industry Ministers. It was a momentous day that changed the history of the Korean economy. On March 25, two months later, Hyundai Ulsan shipyard had a ground-breaking ceremony. At that time many felt that this business was reckless. However, as of 2010, Korea stood tall as the number one ship-building country in the world.

The First Ten-Year Forest Rehabilitation Plan

The forest-reclamation project starting in 1973 was called "The First Ten-Year Forest Rehabilitation Plan" in title. There is a need to note this name. The names "forest reclamation" and "fuel-wood forest establishment", used for the previous ten years, were changed to "forest rehabilitation". This meant a fundamental change in the tree-planting project. The basic direction was set organized by Goh-Kun, Saemaul Director, Ministry of Home Affairs (later prime minister), and included six basic plans.

1. Finishing forest rehabilitation of the whole country within ten years
2. Planting trees with participation of the whole nation
3. Raising tree seedlings using Saemaul organizations to promote village's income
4. Each institution planting trees at assigned regions, taking charge of post-management
5. The Fuel-wood forest establishment project being performed preferentially by each village for self-sufficiency in fuel wood
6. Keeping a thorough control over forest offenses, including illegal cutting, by mobilizing the police organization, and aiming at perfection in forest protection

A detailed plan to move forward was set up by the Forest Service. To achieve the supreme goal of complete tree planting and protection, the responsibility and authority of mayors and county heads were strengthened. The plan included the following:

1. For ten years (1973-1982), 2.1 billion trees will be planted on a total of 1,000,000 ha. (Author's note: South Korea's total forest area was 6,650,000 ha at that time.)

2. For efficiency of nursery practice, the existing forty-two recommended species shall be standardized into the following ten major tree species for intensive planting: Timber trees (Korean white pine, Japanese larch, Sugi, Hinoki), fast-growing trees (Italian poplar, *Populus alba* x *gladulosa*, paulownia, black locust, alders), and nut trees (chestnut). Additionally, for the southern region, bamboos are planted in agreement with warm climates as well as persimmon and walnut trees for food.
3. Fast-growing trees and timber trees shall be in a ratio of seven to three.
4. A Saemaul village nursery is recommended for developing cooperative spirit, and all the planting stocks produced will be bought by the state to contribute to the village's income and be planted in neighboring villages to save transportation cost and time.
5. Only farm houses participating in establishing fuel-wood forests will be allowed to gather fuel wood in a designated place.
6. A national tree planting period shall be set from March 21 to April 20.

Photo 65. At the crossroads of Gwanghwamun with the heaviest traffic in Seoul, used to hang an arch for publicizing national tree planting period for over a month each year.

From the details above only, it might seem that these plans could have been set up by any other regime in history. A closer look, however, reveals that the Ministry of Home Affairs made a methodical, organized, and detailed guide. That is, under the five-step process of the national tree-planting project, the tree-planting process was announced step by step while officials published an easy guidebook and instructed the farmers with this guidebook as well. The steps were as follows:

Step 1: Selection of reserved land for reforestation
Step 2: Preliminary tree-planting instruction to the residents of
    relevant region
Step 3: Preparation for tree seedlings and materials
Step 4: Tree-planting work
Step 5: Inspection of planted trees and tree cares year round

Also of note is that planting and managing of trees were established in a triad system. As shown in the diagram below, tree planting and post-management were placed under the charge of the local government (governor, mayor and county head), protective control under the police, and technical guidance under the forestry officials. The past practice of planting shoddily before and after Arbor Day and managing carelessly was replaced by the establishment of a thorough plan, and a system for post-management, guidance, supervision, and responsibility to prevent any leakage in the project.

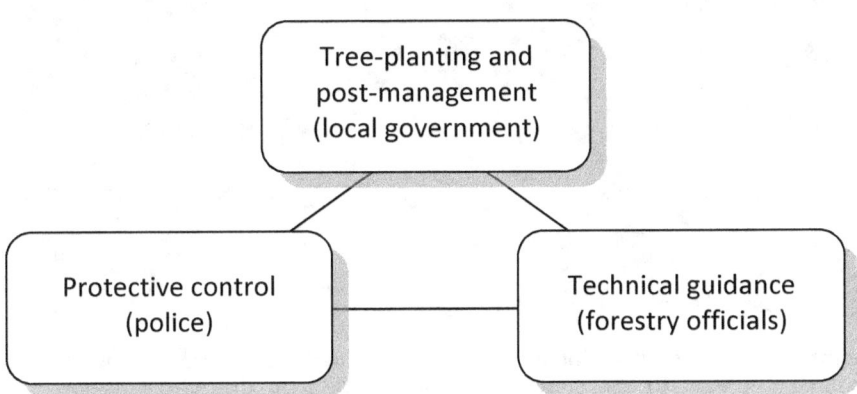

Now the tree-planting project became an operation that made the most of expertise and maximized efficiency. Worthy of special mention is the introduction of responsibility system to ensure the complete protection of forests. That is, the mayor or county head was to be dismissed if over 100 ha of forest land were burned when a forest fire broke out. It was an oppressive guideline, but it had a significant effect.[1]

The method of apportioning budgets was different, too. At that time, the Park Chung-Hee government was enforcing a "planned budget system", which was allocating budgets according to productivity and efficiency. It was a modernized concept of a budget compilation system that had been executed by the US Army, which was learned by a number of our military commanders and officers when they studied in the United States. President Park, too, learned this system directly in the United States for six months in 1954, right after being promoted to brigadier general. Naturally, from that May 16 Revolution on, each ministry had established the planning office and American-style budget system of apportioning budgets based on evaluating business results in advance.

Photo 66. The tree-planting event with a new name of "national tree planting" soon changed into the concept of participation by the whole nation with active enforcement of reforestation by every workplace.

According to this particular concept of budget planning, the Forest Service's "Ten-Year Forest Rehabilitation Plan" wouldn't have been approved for money because it was an investment for a distant future with uncertain economic outcomes. However, forest reclamation was given priority, almost as great as the Saemaul Movement in budget allocations, possibly because it was a project of the president's special strong will.

At last, "The First Ten-Year Forest Rehabilitation Plan" was established. On March 24, Kim Hyun-Ok, Minister of Home Affairs, in charge of this project, introduced this plan in an Emergency Cabinet Meeting. At that time under the Yushin Constitution system, an Emergency Cabinet Meeting was the supreme legislative organ of the country with the Assembly and Cabinet combined. Minister Kim Hyun-Ok, who reported a voluminous project plan in just twenty-four days after the Forest Service fell into his jurisdiction, added this: "I will lead the Saemaul Movement combined with forest rehabilitation by fully mobilizing Home Affairs officials, preventing illegal cutting by mobilizing the police, and fulfilling the project by keeping control over forest offenses."

There was one interesting thing to note. It was March 24 that this "plan" was passed through the Emergency Cabinet Meeting. But Minister Kim Hyun-Ok gathered hundreds of people, including provincial governors, mayors, county heads, police chiefs, and forest-related officials around the country, in the large Home Affairs assembly room on March 16, eight days earlier, to provide instructions on the "Ten-Year Forest Rehabilitation Plan". This means that he started its execution even before the original bill got through the legislative branch with a very rigorous atmosphere as having been said. So it was clear how intensely this operation would be unfolded and with a speed that no one could have imagined then.

Emphasizing that "first is mountain and second is mountain" and that "first is Saemaul and second is Saemaul", Minister Kim made this speech:

> Forest rehabilitation and the Saemaul Movement are equally important.........I want you to bear in mind that the best way for tree-planting and reforestation with the least amount of money is enforcing restricted areas on the mountains. If people are banned from going into a mountain, trees in it will naturally produce seeds and raise their offspring........ You must perceive that this is a shortcut that can make mountains and forests green in the nearest future by a more frugal means.

In addition, to police chiefs he said, "Catching an illegal cutter in the mountains is just as important as catching a thief breaking into a home. If you neglect this, I will charge you with irresponsibility." Whether these words turned out to be nothing but a bluff or a serious threat would become evident by watching the transformation of this project. On this day, Sohn, Head of the institution, presented a detailed propulsion plan in person. The meeting is said to have continued over two hours, and considering the scope of attendance or number of the audience, it seems to have been a meeting that treated the participants "roughly".

There was a procedure for administering "an oath of practice", in which Minister Kim had all participants call the tune, "Let's go to the mountains singing the national anthem", his slogan for the reforestation project. It must have been a noise that could demolish the building. It is said that this slogan followed Minister Kim from then on like a nickname. The instruction didn't end there. After the meeting, each province was required to have a follow-up meeting to transfer the Minister Kim's message to the officials under its supervision.

Photo 67. While most poplars grow well only on the level land with much moisture, the Hyun poplar was an ground-breaking tree species to be planted up on mountain slopes (place marked with a dotted line).

As soon as he proceeded to his post of Forest Service Head, Sohn Soo-Ik was asked by president to set up a gigantic project called "First Ten-Year Forest Rehabilitation Plan". It is no exaggeration that Sohn became the planner and executive of the "10-year plan" from the very first day in his new post. After the new assignment, he devised his own strategy of tree-planting through a quick understanding of his duties. It was a preeminent strategy, even when considered forty years later, and how much more excellent an idea at that time. Here's a summary of the Head of Forest Service Sohn's strategy:

First, we should plant trees in the hearts of the people. Only when the people's hearts are made green can the mountains be made green. To that end, the project should be preceded by providing people with the motivation to participate voluntarily.

Second, the concept of diligence, self-reliance, and cooperation advocated by the Saemaul Movement is the spirit needed for forest reclamation. Introducing these concepts into the forest-reclamation project would make it easier for the entire people to participate in planting trees. We need to put Saemaul organizations to use.

Third, as a village plants more trees, more benefits should go to the village, and this policy should be made known fully in advance.

Fourth, activate a village nursery. To reforest one million ha for ten years will take a tremendous quantity of planting stocks, and the only solution is raising young trees by the village. Making 5,700 village nurseries around the country will ready a mass-production system. Cuttage nursery (for the Italian poplar, and the Hyun poplar) that needs little technique will be covered by village nurseries. In this case, rent for needed land will be supported by the state while materials and fertilizers for nursing seedlings will be provided as a loan. All the seedlings produced this way shall be purchased by the state at the same price as purchased by the commercial nurseries, paying sufficient prices for the farmers' efforts.

Fifth, by holding a "village nursery contest", villages that have successfully cultivated seedlings will be given many benefits to induce a goodwill competition among villages.

Sixth, each province will establish a new Forest Bureau, and each city and county a new Forest Section, which will guarantee the same opportunity for promotion as the other officials lifting their spirits. This will provide incentives for devoted service.

Seventh, during the one-month period of national tree-planting, the national tree-planting headquarters will guide and supervise tree-planting events across the country. This will get rid of the idea that tree-planting is a one-time event and will raise efficiency.

Eighth, make sure of both assigned areas of reforestation and the number of planted seedlings all year round through thorough checks on the sites. This information will serve as basic data of evaluation for relevant officials.

Photo 68. In 1973, on the first Arbor Day after the Forest Service transferred to the Ministry of Home Affairs, President Park (center with no hat) planted trees in Namyangju-gun, Gyeonggi-do. The same day he promised the green rivers and mountains ten years later to youths of the Korean Residents Association in Japan, whose promise was kept after all.

The Arbor Day event of this year was different from a normal year. Nationwide tree-planting events proceeded in good order at each region, and the event hosting the president was held at Migeum-myeon, Yangju-gun, Gyeonggi-do. It was a mammoth event with two thousand people in attendance, with VIPs of three branches of government. He delivered a message of hope to one hundred adolescents under the Korean Residents Association in Japan saying, "You will see green rivers and forests when you come to the home country ten years from now." They planted 6,800 trees in a forest of 13 ha with tree species of

Populus alba x *glandulosa*, Korean white pines, and chestnut trees.

On this day, each ministry of the government and every city, county, Eup, and Myeon nationwide planted trees in 2 to 5 ha, while each class of schools planted in 1.5 ha, and military units also planted trees in their neighborhoods. This way, in the spring of 1973, 297 million trees were planted on over 110,000 ha of forest across the country.

Solution of Farm Village Fuel Wood

The farm villages' fuel-wood shortage problem is closely related to the success of forest rehabilitation. Until the middle of the 1960s, most homes around the country wholly depended on charcoal or firewood for cooking or heating. Without any other type of fuel, people had to rely on forest products. Therefore, regimes in history established fuel-wood forests assiduously so that the fuel supply to the whole nation might not be cut off for any reason. If the fuel supply was cut off, it would be a real disaster. For lack of capability, however, Rhee Syng-Man's government failed to meet the need of a fuel-wood forest, which made the mountains and forests even more desolate.

Park Chung-Hee's administration established fuel-wood forests more assiduously. Even in the one year of 1967, the seventh year of Park's administration that saw the launch of the Forest Service, people planted nearly 1.5 billion trees in fuel-wood forests covering 360,000 ha around the country. At that time, South Korea's land area was 9,920,000 ha, of which forest area was around 6,600,000 ha. And the fuel-wood forest area that could cover all the fuel wood for the farmhouses of the entire country was 1,100,000 ha. Thus it is evident how many fuel-wood forests were created in a year. It was a desperate effort. Officials selected tree species with high ability to produce new shoots when the lower stem was cut off, such as the black locust, alder, *Lespedeza*, and pitch pine. They were tree species far from being used for high quality timber for construction or furniture, but were suitable as fuel wood.

President Park wasn't distracted by such contradictory situations. He started with a conceptual shift. Why must we use a tree for fuel? Isn't there a better fuel? This started the policy of increasing coal production in the middle of the 1960s. Coal was a fuel more useful than wood. In addition, sufficient deposits of coal in Korea for the use of the whole nation could have been another good reason for the fuel shift.

Photo 69. Though village people were mobilized for establishing fuel-wood forests, voluntary cooperation was led by keeping residents not in participation from gathering fuel wood.

In the latter part of the 1960s firewood as fuel started to be replaced by briquettes (nineteen-holed briquettes) in our country. Helped by President Park's encouragement at the beginning of the 1970s, around ten million tons of coal were produced annually, which had already shifted the fuel system of large cities mostly into briquettes. In those days, twelve million tons of briquettes was the amount necessary for the cooking and heating needs of the whole country without using firewood at all. However, the farm villages had trouble because even at the beginning of the 1970s it was impossible to transport briquettes to farm villages because of the poor roads. Paths were too narrow for trucks, and even when using a handcart, briquettes were broken because of the uneven paths. This was before the Saemaul Movement began.

All the same, establishing fuel-wood forests in 1973 was less imperative. Because of increased coal production, only 2.8 million of the total 5.86 million households required fuel wood. Putting annual consumption per household at 4.2 tons, total annual consumption was around 12 million tons, of which around 7 million tons was pure forest fuel, and the rest was agricultural by-products or other fuel. In addition, of around 7 million tons of pure forest fuel, 43 percent was covered by felling, pruning, and thinning of the forest. Therefore, the total forest fuel the government really had to supply annually was around 4 million tons. Because 900,000 ha of the fuel-wood forests had already been established, additional fuel-wood forests needed to supply fuel wood to the farmers in the whole country were only 200,000 ha. Thus the government established a plan of 207,773ha for the next ten years. [1]

There is one thing to add. It is control on entering a mountain area. When he presented the "10-year plan" at the Emergency Cabinet Meeting in March, 1973, Kim Hyun-Ok, Minister of Home Affairs, pushed forward a complete ban on entering mountain areas. However, the ban was mitigated to "control on entering a mountain areas" after being faced by some state ministers' opposition that such an extreme measure could cause many problems. Thus for the purpose of gathering fuel wood, individuals entering the forests were banned most of the year, but village people were allowed to gather fuel wood jointly in July and August. And entering the national and public forests was banned, while private forests were open or controlled by owners. Control on entering mountain areas was certainly credited for forest reclamation. As mentioned by Minister Kim Hyun-Ok, control on entering mountain areas was literally a frugal, efficient way to protect forests. In fact the Saemaul Movement helped to supply coal to villages as a substitute fuel, which facilitated further forest protection.

Photo 70. From a successfully established black locust fuel-wood forest, it was possible to gather fuel wood from four years later on.

Looking back on 1973, there is an event we cannot simply overlook.[18] The price of crude oil soared to four times its value in four months due to the fourth Middle East war in October 1973. It is called the second oil shock. It caused price fluctuation and commodity fluctuation in our country, too, and the government struggled to minimize the damage tightening the reins of expenditure, such as the campaign of saving energy by 10 percent. However, President Park didn't put any limits on expenditure for the forest rehabilitation project and had it go without a hitch as planned.

Chapter 14. Minister of Home Affairs and Head of the Forest Service

Minister of Home Affairs with Infinite Passion

As the First Ten-Year Forest Rehabilitation Plan was published, Minister Kim Hyun-Ok went to the Forest Service every morning during the national tree-planting period (March 21 to April 20) to check the reforestation efforts. It was extremely unusual for a minister to do so. He would crack a joke with encouragement: "I am Minister of Forestry and Jung Seong-Mo, vice-minister, is minister of security."[23]

Because of the careful concern of Minister Kim, the conservation of river and forest projects were upgraded to the most important national policy tasks, together with the Saemaul Movement project, the core project of the Yushin (revitalizing reform) system. The Forest Service Head came to sit spontaneously in both Emergency Cabinet Meetings and Saemaul Cabinet Meetings, resulting in smooth cooperation with related ministries for budgets.

Additionally, by special order, Minister Kim installed "police automatic phone" at the Forest Service. In those days, communications infrastructure was so lacking across the country that even a newspaper company that published a nationwide daily paper had only a few telephone circuits. Even government institutions had to wait for half an hour or so after getting approval and then applying for a long-distance call. In these times, it was possible to pick up the phone and dial a number in person to make an instant long-distance call. Thus how could one describe in words the convenience and promptness? You could imagine how delighted forestry officials were. (This automatic phone, however, was disconnected in 1987, when the Forest Service was returned to the Ministry of Agriculture and Forestry.)

Minister Kim also placed a superintendent of police headquarters in the Forest Service to have him exclusively in charge of forest offenses. He must have wanted to see the last of illegal cutters. With such exceptional consideration of Minister Kim, the Forest Service was transformed into an authoritative upper institution in the eyes of the Ministry of Home Affairs officials around the country. It can be said that he made a foundation of enabling 200 percent achievement of conservation of river and forest projects by lifting the spirits of forestry officials as much as possible. Such achievements are not made by the president, but only a general with excellent leadership skills can achieve them.

Photo 71. Minister Kim had much interest in improvement of traditional farm house furnaces that burned fuel in an inefficient way. He asked the relevant department to device a new type of furnace to reduce fuel consumption.

Minister Kim created the phrases "Absolute Tree-planting" and "Restricted Area" in person to put in the right places. He also asked to improve the furnaces in farm villages to reduce consumption of fuel wood and even urged people to get along by heating only one room. These things made some people criticize him for excessive devotion. He also wrote the famous slogan "Let's go to the mountain singing national anthem". It seems like an attempt to plant a love of mountains and trees in the hearts of the people. It was said that when he used this slogan for the first time, sounds of laughter were heard from here and there. In less than a couple months, however, this song turned into a cheerful slogan. Love of mountains and trees must have settled down in their hearts.

Another effective idea Minister Kim came up with was "planted tree inspections". The idea was to have many supervision teams check in person the actual condition of planted trees at various sites year round after initial reports by local governments of planted quantities in the spring. This supervisory system for preventing weak or false reports he asked officials to call "planted tree inspection".

Needless to say, it is a totally new word (檢木) we cannot see in a Korean or Chinese dictionary. A "Planted tree inspection" was primarily performed at a province and secondarily at the Forest Service. More than two dozen forestry officials for planted tree inspections were selected from each province. Then Minister Kim created a system to exclude any favoritism using cyclic inspection. For example, officials from Gangwon Province engaged in inspecting the actual condition of planted trees in Jeonbuk Province.[1] In fact, there remains a record for the year of 1974 indicating that "planted tree inspections" were performed tree by tree for a total of 310 million trees at 27,000 sites around the country. With the aid of this year-round inspection system, the average survival rates of the planted trees reached over 90 percent during the six years of the reforestation project.

Photo 72. Troika of successful forest reclamation – Park Chung-Hee (right side on the wall in a frame), Kim Hyun-Ok (center) and Sohn Soo-Ik (right) – appear simultaneously (Scene of Kim Hyun-ok, Minister of Home Affairs, announcing the First Ten-Year Forest Reclamation Plan)

Also, Minister Kim established an efficient countermeasure for forest fires. To those engaged in a forest-reclamation project, there is nothing so sorrowful as a forest fire because it blows away in a moment what thousands of people have accomplished over a long period. Natural disasters may be regarded as inevitable, but forest fires are usually man-made disasters. For this reason, the more prevention, the more fruition it returns. Unfortunately, in the past no one had been held responsible for forest fires.

For prevention of forest fires, Minister Kim made the most of the Ministry of Home Affairs organizations. He thought that the fundamental way of preventing a forest fire was to introduce a responsibility system. He made guidelines for asking for responsibility according to the burned area. In case of a large fire with over 100 ha burned, he charged a mayor or a county head with responsibility, hoping that all the officials and police might be mobilized to fight the forest fire in an early stage.

In addition, Minister Kim took the initiative in control of pine caterpillars. From the 1970s forest pests ran to the extreme. Pine caterpillars, pine gall midges, and fall webworms were rampant all over the country. Roadside trees and park trees without exception got holes on the leaves by damage from fall webworms. Trees in the mountains went brownish from damage by pine gall midges. In the summer of 1973, while Minister Kim went to the countryside for inspection of the flood area, he saw pine caterpillars wriggling in a house with flood damage. Upon returning to Seoul, the concerned Kim gave the head of the Forest Service a rigid order to report the actual state of damages around the country and to set up a certain measure of controlling them. When for this purpose, Sohn, Head of the Forest Service, requested a prevention budget of 500 million won (US $1.25million), the Minister unexpectedly supported the total amount.

This was not all. Minister Kim designated the five major forest diseases and insect pests as the pine caterpillar, the pine gall midge, the fall webworm, the alder leaf beetle, and the white pine blister rust. Also making a chart of life cycles, times for control, methods of control, and person in charge of control for each pest, he gave instructions to each provincial governor, mayor, county head, chief of Eup, Myeon, and Dong (township) of the country. He also asked that the head of each institution should peruse and review at all times the instruction chart, which should be kept on the middle of his desk. On the other hand, he entrusted the Forest Service with the duty of making sure and directing that the minister's order was implemented properly by the front institutions. Minister Kim, like President Park, was also an expert at not allowing the disregard of his orders.

In accordance with this, the Forest Service held a Forest Disease and Insect Control Rally by region in an effort to increase self-awareness while performing itinerant demonstrations training for each city and province. It also became an opportunity to increase the effect of insect control and to evaluate the performance accurately. The institution was also asked for daily reports to the Forest Service on the results of insect control.

Photo 73. Kim Hyun-Ok, Minister of Home Affairs, made a new word of "planted tree inspection" to be performed throughout the year to make sure of the result of tree-planting in the spring (June 8, 1973, Planted tree inspection meeting, Forest Experiment Station).

Here is an episode that cannot be laughed off. When President Park attended a local event, the Ministry of Home Affairs always checked in advance the roads on the expected course of movement. On the road from Jeonju to Jinan, Jeonbuk Province, alders planted on cut slope on the roadside had turned brownish from leaf beetle damage. Most alders planted in large numbers for erosion control work in many places had so much damage from leaf beetles that it was well noticeable from a distance. It was clear that Minister Kim would be rebuked if President Park saw these wormed trees. Regardless of this, Minister Kim himself didn't permit such a sight and would issue an impetuous order.

The local officials knew well the dispositions of their superiors. Alder beetles usually eat the lower portion of the tree crown. So along the road of president's procession, officials cut off the lower branches of alders to cover up the damage temporarily. Resembling a woman's legs much exposed, the Head Sohn Soo-Ik said, "It looks like a miniskirt", and soon it was said that the front officials called it "a miniskirt insect control". [1] It showed a humor they didn't lose in spite of their hard work.

Minister Kim's rigorous orders and checks brought about side effects, too. The policy of absolute restriction of entering a mountain area raised disfavor among peasants. He must have been embarrassed because they had followed him so well. He overlooked the fact that the harsh punishment on entering the mountain area was making innocent peasants lawbreakers. It was too much to deprive them of a legal opportunity to gather wild edible greens and fuel wood. Therefore, the strong restriction and punishment at the beginning showed some flexibility later.

In other words, regarding the supply of fuel wood, people were allowed with flexibility to access certain areas of forest under the responsibility of a mayor and county head. In addition, pruning and thinning to obtain fuel wood were allowed but with a strict limit. Woodlots with extremely poor trees were cut down to be replaced with improved tree species. And felled trees were made to use as fuel wood. In no case, however, was gathering leaf litter allowed, because leaf litter increases soil fertility, and has big effects on preventing floods, drought, and free movement of soil on a slope.

Minister Kim Hyun-Ok and the author have a particular personal relationship. In 1969, the author was a tutor to Minister Kim's second son. At that time, the author was attending the Department of Forestry at Seoul National University, and Minister Kim was Seoul mayor. Mayor Kim returned home late at night finishing his duty and sometimes invited the author to his library. He showed a keen interest in my major of forestry and consequently in desolate mountains and forests.

At that time, one of my teachers was Dr. Hyun Shin-Kyu. He emphasized often the importance of leaf litter. "The biggest reason why Korea's mountains are desolate and hard to recover is people's raking up leaf litter from the mountains. Since leaf litter decomposes slowly to release mineral nutrients and makes soil fertile, raking it up is like drawing out blood from a patient inflicted with a serious disease. Therefore, for forest reclamation, banning gathering leaf litter is no less important than planting trees diligently." So the author also stressed the topic to Mayor Kim many times.

Later, while I was studying in the United States, Mayor Kim became Minister of Home Affairs. At that time, he was so devoted to his duty of forest reclamation that he earned the nickname of "Forestry Minister" and especially forbade "gathering leaf litter" by mobilizing police forces. You can imagine how my heart was satisfied to hear the news. This reminds me that human relations are something quite delicate.

Head of the Forest Service, a Genius of Planning

Now it's time to talk about Sohn Soo-Ik, Head of the Forest Service. Let's hear an episode directly from him when Governor Sohn received an official announcement of appointment as Forest Service Head. [11]

"On January 16, 1973, I received an official announcement of appointment to the Forest Service after working as Gyeonggi-do governor. It was not only totally unexpected, but I felt somewhat sorry for it. Though I had advance notification through Kim Hyun-Ok, Minister of Home Affairs a week before, neither Minister Kim nor Kim Bo-Hyeon, Minister of Agriculture and Forestry, knew the reason because it was the president's volition. This was the day of the new-year inspection of the Ministry of Agriculture and Forestry, so I received a certificate of appointment from Prime Minister Kim Jong-Pil and met the president. "I heard that you complained about being the Forest Service Head, didn't you?" To the president's words I said, "No, I didn't. I will do my best." but still I was not persuaded why I had to be Forest Service Head. Soon the president issued an order to set up a mid- to long-term plan for forest

reclamation as soon as possible. Now I reckoned and was reminded of the public promise in his new-year press meeting announced several days ago that he would make the country green within ten years. So I made "the First Ten-Year Forest Rehabilitation Plan" in cooperation with the Saemaul team of the Ministry of Home Affairs.
11)

Inferring from Head Sohn's testimony, it seemed that President Park had set his eyes early enough on Sohn Soo-Ik as Head of the Forest Service. The reason might well be that Sohn had innovated Gyeonggi-Chuncheon's main roadside well above expectations when he was Regional Director of Home Affairs (See Part 3). Of course, the president might have had his eye on him while he was working at the Blue House. But it is too much that the president officially announced his appointment as Forest Service Head, no more than a vice-minister level, although he was capable enough to be a minister. The president could not have been ignorant of this context, so he must have been thinking of some proper compensation on his own.

President Park first transferred the Forest Service from the Ministry of Agriculture and Forestry to the Ministry of Home Affairs, one month after officially announcing the appointment of Sohn Soo-Ik as Forest Service Head. The ministry was to have the soil ready that could drive forest rehabilitation strongly by mobilizing the Ministry of Home Affair's administrative, police, and financial power. In addition, the president accepted Sohn's proposal for expanding the forestry administrative organization and promotion of officials one hundred percent as requested.

Sohn, Head of the Forest Service, picked his way forward in this way. First, he set up the concept of "national tree planting'" which came from the idea that without all the people's participation and support, it was difficult to make a green country quickly. Accordingly, a one-day tree-planting on Arbor Day was now regarded as insufficient, so a month was set for planting from March 21 as the "National Tree-planting Period". Putting up a large placard reading "Mountain-mountain-mountain, Tree-tree-tree" in the cross section of Gwanghwamun, the busiest street in Seoul, was to propose "national tree-planting" to the entire nation.

Second, the seedlings must be grown with the spirit of self-reliance and cooperation. Securing the fuel wood for a farm village is the prerequisite for forest reclamation. Thus, Fuel-wood forests should be established as much as needed, but seedlings should be raised in Saemaul, a body of practice for self-reliance and cooperation. And the seedlings produced should be bought by the government at market price to promote income for the farmers.

Third, the ratio of fast-growing trees to slow-growing timber trees should be seven to three. At the beginning of the 1970s, mountains in our country were still desolate due to continuous washing out of top soil by pouring rain and by the reckless collection of leaf litter. Therefore, in those days, it was the top priority to plant trees with 1) good survival on infertile soil, 2) fast growth, 3) soil improving ability, 4) high resistance to diseases and insect pests, and 5) potential for fuel-wood production as much as possible and as early as possible.

Reforestation is called a far-sighted national policy. It is desirable to plant timber trees with large economic value to secure long-term forest resources. However, in our circumstances, we needed to worry about firewood for the coming winter and frequent flooding during the rainy season in summer. It was impossible to insist on timber trees only. The mountains themselves were too sterile for timber trees to grow well. To meet such national requirements, it was planned to plant initially 1) fast-growing trees such as *Populus alba* x *glandulosa*, Italian poplar, and paulownia, and 2) black locust or alder that made mountain areas fertile by converting atmospheric nitrogen into nitrogen fertilizer, with wide, extended roots and that had strong sprouting ability.

Fourth, focus was also placed on the erosion-control project, which was as urgent as reforestation. The total area of wasteland (land in need of urgent erosion control) that reached 449,483 ha in 1961 at the time of the military revolution had continued to decrease in the meantime to 84,220 ha in 1973. Erosion-control projects were planned to focus on the following areas, such as Yeoju and Icheon district in Gyeonggi-do, Yesan in Chungnam, Iksan in Jeonbuk, Gokseong in Jeonbuk, etc.

Not long after Sohn, Head of the Forest Service, had proceeded to his post, there was an episode between President Park and Sohn over a helicopter. Let's hear it directly from Sohn. [11]

"Performing forest administration essentially takes a helicopter.

When I was transferred to the Forest Service, there had been three helicopters, which I think I have used effectively. Incidentally, not long after I was moved to the Forest Service, the president said, "Do you want to have an additional helicopter?" So I said, "No. We have helicopters ourselves." But after some time, the president asked me again, 'Do you want to have an additional helicopter?' The president presumably remembered my previous response, so I wondered why he asked the same question twice. I realized that he was ordering me to helicopter here and there to check the plantations. Then I received the helicopter gratefully. After that, for six years in the post of the Forest Service, I flew diligently in a helicopter for almost six hundred hours, threading my way around the mountains and fields of my mother country. This sometimes caused the front officials to come running hurriedly, taking my helicopter for the president's. It seems that I have not been a welcome guy for mayors, county heads, and police chiefs around the country." [11]

Nowadays, there are around fifty helicopters in Forest Service, which are used effectively and appropriately for fighting forest fires, controlling pests, and monitoring mountains and forests. Helicopters have been a necessity also in transporting seedlings, materials, reforestation personnel, and the like to high mountains without roads opened. The president's question forty years ago, "Do you want to have an additional helicopter?" seems to have provided a preliminary notice about the path for the forest rehabilitation project in the future.

Sohn, Head of the Forest Service, seems to have received many grants from President Park, often and in large amounts. Here is his testimony again. [11]

"The president would give me not a small amount of money for use as an expense account occasionally in spring and autumn with a signed letter of encouragement "Each time I travel, I see the mountains and fields of the mother country getting greener each year......" At one time, along with a signed letter, he gave me an unexpectedly large amount of money. I reluctantly accepted it, saying "Mr. President, you seem to have many uses for money yourself. I have my own expense accounts." He told me that when he was teaching at Mungyeong in the Japanese Colonial era, he was a teacher in charge of a regional forest officer's son, and the officer often bought him rice wine. Then he told me to buy some wine for the front forest officials to encourage them so that they may not be bribed with wine by lumbering men. So I endeavored to make the president's donation reach the forest officials around the country, while I also had some amount of Soju (hard liquor)." [11]

Photo 74. Understanding the importance of a helicopter in the duty of forest reclamation, President Park presented one to Sohn Soo-Ik, Head of the Forest Service. Sohn inspected nurseries and reclamation sites in every corner of the country by helicopter.

Sometimes Sohn made a joke that he had graduated from the department of forestry in Law School. However, this was not just a joke. It is Sohn, Head of the Forest Service, who held a forest owners' contest first in our country. At that time, there were around two million forest owners in the whole country. They are legal owners of a forest. Generally, however, the forest owners did not see how they were related to the tree-planting project. Their general attitude was that it was their forest and that there was nothing for them to do more than gathering fuel wood and choosing a graveyard as they pleased. Sohn realized a need to inspire a love of forests and encouragement in such forest owners. This idea was possible because he was familiar with both law and forestry. Moreover, when national tree planting was pushed forward, it would have been difficult if forest owners had not taken the initiative.

On October 31, 1973, the first mountain owner contest was held in the Chungbuk Cigarette Manufactory Main Hall. It was a large-scale event with attendance of the provincial governor, mayors, county heads, all forestry officials and two thousand forest owners. "Tree-Planting King'" for various species was selected by cities and counties to confer the pennant and cup. The result of the forest owners' contest was reported to the president with munificent support from the government's budget ministry. Then, each year, the forest owners' contest was held taking turns by province. [11]

Chapter 15. Two Sticking Points:
Slash-and-Burn Farmers and Pests

Five-Year Slash-and-Burn Farming Regulation Plan

A Wikipedia entry defines slash-and-burn as follow:

> "Slash-and-burn is an agricultural technique that involves cutting and burning of forests or woodlands to create fields. It is subsistence agriculture that typically uses little technology or other tools. It is typically part of shifting cultivation agriculture. There are an estimated 250 million slash-and-burn farmers across the world. They are chiefly responsible for destroying the virgin forest."

We don't have slash-and-burn farmers now in our country. If there are one or two of them, it would immediately appear in a newspaper or on TV as news. Anyway, these days, even college students don't know what a slash-and-burn farmer is probably because they have never seen the technique, even if they may have heard of it. The author learned about a slash-and-burn farmer at elementary school in my fifth or sixth grade.

This book has referred to slash-and-burn farming regulations in Part 2, and here is a summary of the history of slash-and-burn farming regulation in our country:

1966: Legislated slash-and-burn farming regulation

1967: Installed voluntary report period for slash-and-burn fields. At that time, there were 300,000 households of slash-and-burn farming subject to regulation, but until 1972 the law was not properly in effect for want of budget, management and supervision.

1973: Execution of general survey on current status of slash-and-burn fields in the nation

1974-1978: Established Five-Year Slash-and-Burn Farming Regulation Plan and completed the project in 1978.

Photo 75. Slash-and-burn had been rampant without reach of the law until the beginning of the 1970s. It is sorrowful that damage was on a large scale including forest at a steep slope.

The slash-and-burn farming regulation is basically different from tree-planting or the erosion-control project because it is dealing with people. Slash-and-burn field is a means of the minimum living made by those who have no house, no land and no money, and who go to the mountains. Thus, to prevent a slash-and-burn farming, the state should give land to the farmers or take responsibility for urban resettlement and provision of jobs for these farmers, while taking measures to keep them from returning to the mountain. That is why disrupting slash-and-burn farming is a difficult job. Here's an experience of slash-and-burn farming regulations by Park Soon-Jo at the Forest Service. [1].

" In the spring of 1967, I was officially appointed as Chief of Hwacheon Branch Office under the Seoul Regional Forest Office.

Upon proceeding to my post, I delivered an order of banning slash-and-burns in national forests. In accordance with the national policy, it was an order to get rid of 6,000 pyeong (4.9 acres) of slash-and-burn fields and reforest the same area. Ten households of slash-and-burn farmers protested tearfully. I couldn't do this or that at their complaint of how to make a living. Then, a lucky turn of events came. I became aware that the Ri (village) head in the neighborhood was rice-field farming illegally on 3000 pyeong (2.5 acres) of the state land in the lower village. By using a carrot and stick, I succeeded to lease the rice paddy cultivated by the Ri head by splitting it into units of 200 pyeong (0.16 acres) to slash-and burn farmers as the price for stopping their farming. To them, it was a dream come true to be able to grow rice. After a long time of staple food of potato, corn, and beans, they finally came to enjoy boiled rice. Of course, I fulfilled the reforestation of 6,000 pyeong (4.9 acres) successfully as I had been ordered. I was just lucky after all. Slash-and-burn farming regulation will lead to failure without a substitute."

Photo 76. Slash-and-burn people lived in a shed poorer than a barn, probably due to frequent moves.

They say slash-and-burn farmers first appeared in our country in Joseon era. But in the prevailing view, the Japanese Colonial period is when that its numbers increased rapidly because the Japanese militarists deprived our country of around 50 percent of the forest land area. The only way for farmers who lost their farmland to subsist was probably going into a mountain free of the Japanese militarists' evil hands and turning over slash-and burn fields. Slash-and-burn fields were chiefly distributed in the east mountainous area in Gangwon-do and

Chungbuk, the north mountainous areas of Gyeongbuk, and were partially discovered in other areas. Though slash-and-burn farmers have a sad history, they are never to be left alone. It is not only because they are one of the main culprits in destroying mountains and forests, but also because it is not right to allow people to live alienated in the hinterland and failing to receive the state's protection and benefits.

Oddly, there was no countermeasure for slash-and-burn farmers included in the first stage of the Saemaul Movement or even in the First Ten-Year Forest Rehabilitation Plan. It seems that either the Forest Service had omitted addressing the problem or officials worried about enforcement taking a bad turn. As if to prove the truth of this fear, bad things soon did happen.

Photo 77. When deporting slash-and-burn people, officials accompanied them to the last moment with a thorough supervision by over three years of recording on paper so that they might not return to slash-and-burn farming.

It was on June 1, 1973, about three months after the Ten-Year Forest Rehabilitation Plan entered into enforcement. While inspecting on the reserved land for Yeongdong Expressway in a helicopter, President Park caught the sight of slash-and-burn in Hoengseong and Pyeongchang, Gangwon-do. To President Park, who was strongly driving forward the Farmers' Income-Boosting Project and Forest Rehabilitation Project, a slash-and-burn field must have seemed an intolerable sight and an obstacle to both projects. Furthermore, President Park had thought that the Slash-and-Burn Farming Regulation Project, which had started in

1967, was coming to a close.

Returning to Seoul, President Park immediately issued an order. "Establish a plan to clear off the slash-and-burn fields by prioritizing a complete ban of farming on steep slopes. A policy should be set up to stabilize the livelihood of slash-and-burn farmers by other means." Simultaneously, President Park advanced a measure for delivering a special subsidy of 100 million won (US $250,000) to Gangwon-do. This gave birth to the Five-Year Slash-and-Burn Farming Regulation Plan (1974-1978).

Clearance of the slash-and-burn farmers was connected to national security. Since slash-and-burn farmers lived in the hinterland of the mountains, they were helpless against Red guerillas who might appear. The government couldn't simply leave them alone, so surveys of the actual condition of slash-and-burn farmers was made. Two-hundred eighty thousand households were getting along using slash-and-burn fields on a total area of 124,000 ha, averaging 0.44 ha per household.

First, the Forest Service prepared criteria for regulating slash-and-burn fields. On the basis of the mountain gradient, 20° or over were all made forest. Slash-and-burn fields under 20° were accepted as an arable land. Slash-and-burn people were classified into three groups based on their desire; local settlement, residence in the neighborhood, or a complete move. [1]

"Local settlement" was the case for farms on gentle slopes under 20°, and these were officially permitted to go on farming on the same place. Those classified as "Residence in the neighborhood" were helped in locating a village neighboring the slash-and-burn area, and a subsidy was given to build a house and a loan was provided to raise Korean cows, cultivate pasture, nurse tree seedlings, and make a mulberry field. If they wanted, they received assistance in changing their occupation. Those classified as "Complete move" left the mountains and moved to a city where they received special service from the state, which was fully responsible for their move.

Receiving the president's instruction, Sohn, Head of the Forest Service, established a cautious and circumspect plan for regulating slash-and-burn people. It is the "Guide to Office Routine of Slash-and-Burn Regulation". [1] The main contents are as follows:

1. If one removes his house willingly and moves to a village, 400,000 won (US $1,003) shall be provided in aid for moving expenses per household. This sum will be paid in two installments, the first being 130,000 won (US $326).

2. If, after removing a house, the resident plants trees on the house lot, it shall be regarded as giving up slash-and-burn farming.

3. For a slash-and-burn farmer to move, a related official shall ride along in the moving truck and will be responsible for ushering the farmer to the destination. Cities or counties that are subject to receiving the farmer shall arrange a job and visit him periodically to make sure he has no difficulty in urban living. If the resident moves to another place again, an official should attach a individual record for three years to make sure the farmer does not return to slash-and-burn farming.

4. Other settlement support policy: support a loan to arrange for the resident to start a farming business or enable him to find employment in local public works preferentially.

5. Records of slash-and-burn farming regulations shall be permanent, and "a management map of Eup and Myeon without slash-and-burn fields" shall be prepared to hang on the office wall for continuous management.

6. Develop a thorough air-surveillance system to keep the farmer from going back to the mountain or to cultivation, and to execute planting trees immediately.

7. To make it impossible to manipulate statistics or report falsely, the Forest Service, Regional Forest Office, County office, and police station shall be collectively responsible, checking and reporting on the site once or twice a year.

8. Hold a provincial slash-and–burn farming regulation contest annually to inspire a sense of mission in related officials and encourage them to achieve the project without failure.

9. Such supervisory systems shall be continued until slash-and-burn farming regulations have been fully completed.

Photo 78. Scene of a settlement for slash-and-burn farmers. Though it was a desolate place without a tree in nearby mountains, a school was first built to give education to their children.

The program actually continued until 1979. This kind of thorough progress and careful consideration of the slash-and-burn farmer's position naturally resulted in a great success. Among 283,870 slash-and-burn households, 15,734 moved to cities, 2,349 transferred to a nearby village, 265,787 (around 94%) settled where they used to live. In case of settlement, they were compelled to buy slash-and-burn arable land in redemption by yearly installments. The government grants for this project totaled 12.6 billion won (US $26 million). Today, slash-and-burn fields have disappeared into history. Of the 124,643 ha of slash-and-burn fields, 86,073 ha were restored to mountain forests, and the rest became farm land.

Power of the Pine Gall Midge Smaller Than a Mosquito

Another obstacle to the forest rehabilitation project was the presence of tree insects. Because of pests, we sometimes see such green, beautiful trees wither away to a sickly yellow. The pest has a formidable destructive power that can bring our years of efforts to nothing in just several months. As noted in the previous chapter, what were causing the most fatal damage to forests were pine caterpillars, pine gall midges, fall webworms, alder leaf beetles, and white pine blister rust. Thus the government designated these five as the major diseases and pests. The maxim "knowledge is power" precisely applies to controlling forest pests. Simply understanding the life cycle for each pest, such as egg-laying, hibernating, breeding, and movement can yield quite effective methods for their control.

Kim Hyun-Ok, Minister of Home Affairs, and Sohn Soo-Ik, Head of the Forest Service, are considered to have succeeded in controlling the forest insects. They clearly informed the provincial governors, mayors, county heads, chiefs of Eup, Myeon and Dong (town) about the life cycles, times of control, best methods of control of insects. Accordingly, heads of institutions worked hard to avoid errors by designating persons in charge. They held local "forest insects control rallies" and established insect-control daily report systems.

The most malignant of the five major forest diseases and insects was the pine gall midge. It is a fly smaller than a mosquito. The midge lays eggs on the young needles of a pine tree, and the hatched larvae make a gall in the base of a leaf, leading it to death. It is known to have existed in Korea since the Japanese colonial age, and in the 1970s it began to threaten the pine forests around the country. In Gyeongju, since 1971 the midge had spread rapidly in the area of Mt. Toham. Gyeongju is a millennium-old city with many historical sites, and it was the region in which president Park took particular interest. The Forest Service hurried to dust the area with BHC chemicals using a plane because of the urgent situation. Unexpectedly, however, the dusting had the side effect of damaging neighboring fish, beekeeping, and silk-worm farms. Today, BHC cannot be used because of environmental problems it causes, but in those days it was permitted domestically.

As the damage from pine gall midges became ever worse, a buffer zone (a 4km-wide belt-like clearing of pine forest) was made to stop the gall midge's migration. In the case of Weolseong-gun, Gyeongbuk, around 12,000 ha of pine forest was felled to make a large buffer zone in 40 km long (east to west) and 4 km wide. When the damaged area around the scenic Bukhan River near Seoul was felled to create a buffer zone, it was executed only after obtaining ratification from President Park for fear that it might cause public criticism.

In the 1970s, damage from pine gall midges became ever larger in scale. An effective control method had not yet developed. The Blue House itself came forward and openly accepted applications from all scientific societies and research institutes around the country for effective methods of control. While geneticists proposed breeding sterile midges, the Institute of Atomic Energy Research proposed blocking reproduction by radioactive treatment. Ultimately, the selected method of control was the use of a natural enemy. This method, the most eco-friendly method proposed, was offered by Koh Je-Ho, section chief of the Forest Experiment Station. The technique included artificially breeding and releasing wasps that laid eggs on the larvae of pine gall midges and finally killed them. The project took time, however, it didn't have a rapid effect.

Photo 79. A pine gall midge smaller than a mosquito spread rapidly and severely damages a Korean red pine forest (a photo courtesy of the Forest Research Institute).

Hyeonchung-sa in Asan, Chungnam is where the pine gall midge was controlled successfully. President Park frequented this place because he was a known admirer of Admiral Lee Sun-Shin, who has been enshrined there. At that time, the pine gall midge was rampant in this place. Sohn, Head of the Forest Service, came forward himself. Jeong Jin-Ho, subsection chief of forest section, Asan-gun, Chungnam, was quite familiar with the life cycle of the pine gall midge. That is, he knew the enemy. First, larva of the pine gall midge falls to the ground from a pine needle in late autumn and then hibernates in the ground. Second, the larva, after spending the winter in the ground, hatches into an adult insect between May and July, and then lays eggs on the needles of the pines. The gall midge larva is shaped like a small maggot, is 1 to 2 mm in length, and yellow-colored. Thinking of such a life cycle, Jeong proposed a method of covering the bare ground with polyethylene film. [1]

Polyethylene film is placed on the ground in late autumn, and the larvae would fall on the film, where they could be collected and killed easily. This measure would also have the added effect of obstructing the hatching adults from coming out of the ground in the spring. Sohn, and his staffs accepted this proposal. To lay film around the Hyeonchung-sa, they placed a special order of 16-ton, large-width film from Namhae Chemical Inc. and spread it across 7 ha of the surrounding mountain forests, expending a total of 5 million won (US $10,330). Cheered by collection of six liters of larvae in that autumn, they continued the treatment for three years, which provided significant success in controlling the pine gall midge. [1]

This method was used later to control the same insect in the natural pine forests near Beopju-sa Buddhist temple, Boeun, Chungbuk. Although the pine trees around Gyeongju Bulguk-sa temple were all felled at the beginning by damage from the gall midge, pines in Hyeonchung-sa and Beopju-sa are well preserved even now. This method has worked one hundred percent so far. The Jeongipum Pine on Mt. Sokri, known as the favorite of Koreans, was barely saved by both laying film on the ground and surrounding the whole tree with insect nets for several years (a project in which the author took part).

Photo 80. Sohn Soo-Ik, Head of the Forest Service, is commanding a nationwide campaign exhibition meeting for controlling pine caterpillars himself (May 6, 1975).

The pine gall midge has occupied the Korean Peninsula for half a century. In 1961, it was observed in 410,000 ha (the forest area of South Korea was 6.6 million ha at that time). Since the latter part of 1980s, the entire country, including Mt. Seolak in the north-eastern part of South Korea, has come under its influence, and the infested area reaches 190,000 ha annually. And it has not spared North Korea. The midge has migrated north, passing the DMZ (Demilitarized Zone) and moving all the way up to Hamheung. This means that the pine gall midge has occupied the entire Korean Peninsula.

So far, a number of pine forests have been damaged but the pines remain. At the beginning of the 1970s, we expected that the spread of the gall midge would kill every pine tree in Korea. However, even in extremely damaged area, the gall midge killed only around 30 to 40 percent of the trees. The rest are thriving again. Forests once swept by the pine gall midge have gained the power of resistance. Fortunately, although the gall midge intrudes again about every fifteen to twenty years, the level of damage it causes is diminishing. This case reminds us that the forest's ability to stand on its own and providence of nature are too abstruse for humans to explain with our limited knowledge.

As we solved the two sticking points in forest reclamation, slash-and-burn farmers and forest pests, and waged an all-out war by planting trees continuously, mountains across the country were gradually clothed in green beginning in the late 1970s. As the mountains have slowly recovered, animals in the mountains have also begun to make an appearance. Going to the mountain these days, one can hear every kind of beautiful bird chirping and see cute rabbits and roe deer. Boars have multiplied so much that they hurt the crops and now appear in the middle of cities. This proves that our mountains have grown dense.

Given the poachers' recklessness, since when have there been so many wild animals in the mountains? This phenomena is probably the result of the president's concern about shooting. In the 1960s, when the fields and mountains were bare and when wild animals had disappeared, President Park was already aware of the necessity for protecting wild animals as a way of helping the forests. In particular, mountain birds such as a great tit eat forest vermin and thus contribute to forest reclamation indirectly.

In 1967, when the Forest Service was established, President Park also enacted the "Wildlife Protection and Hunting Law" and regulated indiscriminate fishing. For three years beginning in August 1972, he resolutely carried out the prohibited shooting, and in the face of opposition from hunters, he extended this action in 1975 and 1979. Only sparrows and birds around airports were allowed for hunting. Only in Jeju Island was hunting allowed in order to attract tourists. Though restrictions of shooting were partly relaxed during the 1980s with the introduction of the Circular Hunting System, we can fairly say that President Park has protected Korean wildlife by taking action that was ahead of its time.

Part 5.

Scenic Beauty Restored

Chapter 16. Self-Sufficiency of Rice Achieved

The Farmers' Day Event in Which He Participated for Eighteen Years

Korea used to observe something called "Farmers' Day". This day was first announced on June 15, 1946, after the Liberation. From 1996, however, Farmers' Day was abolished, and instead November 11 was designated as the day to remember farmers and the rice harvest. It gives an impression that this traditional nationwide event, observed since the ancient Shilla Dynasty, has now been reduced to an event only for farmers who account for about six percent of the whole population.

In fact, almost all of Korea's presidents seem to have been quite neglectful of the Farmers' Day. Record shows that they have typically released a statement and had some pictures taken while performing some act to encourage farmers such as standing on the levee of a rice paddy in formal dress and shiny shoes. Having such documentary photographs shows that, as a person in power, they were concerned about food, but nothing more. President Park was the only exception. He showed up at his first Farmers' Day event as leader just twenty-five days after he had succeeded in his military revolution. The event was at a rice paddy in Gimpo, and he planted rice skillfully in a team with the farmers, rolling up his military uniform pants and wearing a straw hat. That was not all. After finishing the rice-planting, he shared in drinking raw rice wine with his coworker farmers on the rice paddy levee.

Photo 81. From the start of his coming into power, President Park had never been absent from the rice-planting event on Farmer's Day.

Some prefer to say that such "performance" was merely a show to draw support for his revolution. But this is not a fair judgment. For eighteen years of his reign, President Park never missed rice planting on Farmers' Day, teaming up with farmers and then sharing raw rice wine with them. It was not a show in the least. His attachment was such that he "attended this event, putting all state affairs aside," according to his secretaries. And it was not just Farmers' Day's. He also never missed participating in the rice-reaping event of the fall season.

So why did the president never miss the opportunity to encourage agriculture in this way? Although some attribute it to his personal memory of poverty in childhood, the real answer lies in later events. In early January 1974, he delivered an order, written in his own handwriting, to relevant ministries: "Achieve self-sufficiency in staple food grains". '

The World's Number One in Productivity of Rice Cultivation

A goal for Rice self-sufficiency? To Koreans living in 2013, such a goal might sound like an issue for some African countries. But as recently as the early 1970s, our country had difficulty for want of food. First, rice, our staple food grain, was in short supply. In 1970, our country's rice production was around 3.9 million tons. Thus, for a population of 31.4 million at that time, we needed around 4.3 million tons of rice annually. We were short about 0.4 million tons for that year. Buying it from a foreign country could be another way to get by, but we had insufficient money for it. What would you do if you were the person in power?

President Park's answer to this question was very simple and fundamental. First, the truly best policy was to increase production. But since increasing farmland overnight is out of the question, he decided to try and increase the harvest per unit area from the existing land as much as possible. Second was the movement for rice saving; sparing rice and eating it in mixture with other cereals as much as possible, until the day we achieve self-sufficiency.

In fact, since the middle of the 1960s President Park had ordered the breeding of a high-yield variety of rice to various institutes. The fruit of this effort was Unification Rice, which Professor Heo Mun-Hoi, Seoul National University, had bred while working jointly with the International Rice Research Institute in the Philippines. It was a real miracle that we succeeded in producing a new variety of rice in just seven years!

Unification Rice has been popularized since 1971. While an ordinary rice plant had 80 to 90 grains, a Unification Rice plant usually had 120 to 130 grains, or even up to 200. In 1974, we had 4.42 million tons of rice production, and harvested 5.19 million tons in 1976 achieving self-sufficiency in rice for the first time. It was a landmark event one of the most significant since Dangun, the founding father of the Korean nation. Subsequently, when Unification Rice was expanded to 55 percent of the total rice cultivation in 1977, Korea harvested 6.01 million tons. Unification Rice, with productivity of $437kg/1,000m^2$, brought a 33 percent increase in harvest compared with ordinary rice, a historic event that established a new world record.

The process of gaining self-sufficiency in staple food grains was never smooth. Until 1975, we continued to be in short supply of rice and had to rely on imports. In 1970, rice prices were over twice as high as that of wheat or barley. Importing barley instead of rice would provide over double the quantities. Therefore, the situation called for eating mixed grains to save the foreign currency. President Park strongly drove a movement for rice saving, even in the face of public criticism. The government enforced regulations on mixing grains. The regulation called for boiled barley and flour-based meals twice a week. This amount was increased to five times a week after 1972. These regulations were accompanied by a widespread crackdown. Administration by "5 percent instruction and 95 percent check" was a skill President Park polished in the army. Squads in disguise raided restaurants and checked by opening the lids of kettles. In schools, teachers checked packed lunches every lunch time to see whether barley was mixed as directed. Needless to say, President Park, who directed this whole process, continued to have grains mixed with barley every day in the Blue House.

Photo 82. President Park (left) enjoyed drinking Makgeoli (liquor made of rice) with farmers after attending the Farmer's Day event.

It was a desperate struggle, but the belief that we should not rely on imports for rice, the staple food of our nation, finally bore fruit. In 2009, rice production reached nearly five million tons and, despite increased population, per capita annual consumption of rice decreased to 74 kg (versus 136 kg in 1970), leaving an annual surplus of nearly a million tons. That has made the government rather encourage raw rice wine, and rice crackers. It is to replace flour wheat, for which we have to rely solely on imports, so our situation has been completely reversed within forty years.

Photo 83. From right after the revolution, President Park showed continued interest in improving a rice cultivar for increased food. He expressed satisfaction, counting up himself the grains of a new high-yield cultivar, "Unification Rice".

Although these days it is said that rice is overproduced, we must consider the importance of self-sufficiency in our food supply, which means the ratio of self-sufficiency by combining rice with other grains, vegetables and stock feed. Owing to the campaign to increase rice production, our country's self-sufficiency in food overall soared to around 80 percent during the 1970s, but then it plummeted to 31 percent in the 1980s, 28 percent in the 1990s and to less than 20 percent today. We now stand third from the bottom among OECD countries. Some answer that we can buy food with money from selling automobiles or televisions even more cheaply than cultivating it on our own farms. That is right by economic logic.

However, At present, the earth has been enslaved by global warming. Each year the mean temperature is rising, desertification goes on in many parts of the globe, accompanied by unusual weather. No one can predict when a global poor harvest of grains will befall us. What is more threatening is the fact that there are always merchants and politicians watching for their chance to exploit a world food crisis.

Photo 84. The farmers planted the new cultivar of "Unification Rice" with joy and big expectation.

This chapter has been concerned with Korea's self-sufficiency in staple food grains because this topic is closely related to forest reclamation and the conservation of rivers and forests. Rice farming is not just about producing things to eat. It performs a great role not only in its traditional functions of preserving the ecosystem, controlling floods, temperature, and humidity, purifying the atmosphere, but also in reducing carbon dioxide, which is a global concern these days. We have touched on rice farming because it has many common points with the functions of forests.

Chapter 17. Country Landscaping Project

Discrimination of a National Leader

"One Monday morning, I was informed that the president wanted to see me, Head of the Forest Service, promptly. When I entered his office, worrying myself about the possibility of rebuke, he put a piece of ruled paper on the meeting table. On it there were instructions coupled with concrete pictures colored with pink, yellow, and green pencils. The text read, 'On the cut slope of Seoul-Busan Expressway, plant forsythia and install landscaping stones. Landscape by planting azaleas and royal azaleas between the stones and plant evergreens like Sargent Juniper or box tree over them.' Forsythia was colored in yellow, azaleas and royal azaleas in pink, and evergreens in green".

Photo 85. President Park had such a deep interest and professional expertise in landscaping that he even made an expressway landscaping plan with his own hand drawing.

The above is recollection by Sohn Soo-Ik.[11] Where there is demand, an industry arises. Until production of automobiles called the 'Pony' in the latter half of the 1970s, we had had almost no automobile-related industry. Since Hyundai Motors Inc. produced the Pony, automobiles have spread to every home until today with many new auto-related industries becoming successful.

A good entrepreneur is a person who starts an enterprise suited for the level of the national income. In the middle of the 1970s, a fitness center called Clark Hatch opened at a hotel in Seoul. However, this fitness club, part of a global chain, closed four years later because at that time our country had a per capita national income of $1,000. There were many undernourished people and few who felt the need for diet or getting in shape. Business was limited to foreign customers who stayed at the hotel.

When can we enjoy a nicely landscaped environment with investment at what amount of national income? Landscape architecture is a little bit different story from forest reclamation and the conservation of rivers and forests. Though they share the use of woody plants as the main ingredient, there is a big difference: while forest reclamation has a direct effect on food and shelter, landscaping is the element that feasts our eyes only after food, clothing, and shelter issues have been resolved.

It is generally accepted that people take a positive interest in landscaping when their national income reaches $10,000. In the case of our country, this level was achieved in the middle 1990s. But in our country, someone started this landscaping project about twenty years earlier than this. This person made an expressway, automobile company, iron company, and shipbuilding company all twenty years earlier, and he initiated the planting of hundreds of millions of trees each year, even when Korea's people had severe difficulty with a food shortage.

The modern landscaping of Korea was not accelerated by private demands, as were the automobile-related industries, but by the government's needs and plans led by President Park. The result was the creation of a new industry. Such is the great difference between an enterprise president and a national leader. While a company president can make a huge success looking five or six years ahead, a national leader should have discrimination for looking twenty or thirty years ahead. By a curious coincidence, President Park was looking twenty or thirty years ahead from nearly all sides. His only mistake was putting democratization on the back burner.

Started the Country Landscaping Even Though Food Was in Short Supply

The record suggests that President Park showed earnest interest in landscaping in 1970, when the Saemaul Movement had not been fueled yet. It was when peasants, accounting for as much as a third of the population, were still short of food and living without electricity in thatched houses with conventional-type smelly toilets. Under these circumstances, it was amazing that he began to conceive of landscaping the whole country. Could President Park have foreseen that around twenty years later our people would yearn for something that feasts our eyes in our leisure? The answer has not been found yet by the author.

In 1970, President Park invited Oh Whee-Young, an expert in landscaping, to give a lecture on landscape architecture. Oh had received a Master's of Science degree in landscape architecture at the University of Illinois in the United States and were working for the Chicago Green Area Administration. In May 1972, Oh Whee-Young was appointed as a secretary in the Blue House for landscaping and construction. It was also at this time that a license system for landscaping construction was introduced. In 1974, for professional landscaping services, Korea Landscape Development Corporation was started as a public enterprise. Until it was privatized, the institution took exclusive charge of large-scale landscaping construction work on highway roadsides, industrial-complex neighborhoods, new dam-construction sites, etc. as ordered by the government.

After 1970, President Park tried systematic scenery landscaping in the construction of highways, factories, national parks, tourist sites, railroads, as well as the process of restoring cultural assets. It was the beginning of the Korea's landscaping. In 1972, he put a landscaping secretariat in the Blue House and led landscaping to be executed according to international standards during the process of the nation's construction. The Blue House published landscaping-related books for use as guidebooks. They are <Guide to Cut Slope Damage Maintenance>,

<Guide to Factory Landscaping>, <Guide to Expressway Functional Tree-Planting><Guide to Railway Landscaping>, among others.

Photo 86. Following President Park's special order, factory landscaping was planned in the direction of caring for the employees' health and welfare (Dongbang Industry, 1978).

President Park also gave instructions to hold a factory landscaping contest between all the factories across the country in an effort to lead a goodwill competition, with its results to be reported to the president. President Park's response to this report instructed landscapers to consider the employees' health and wellbeing rather than to focus on the officers' convenience. Accordingly, factories were designed with lounges and exercise facilities, and landscapers planted trees to absorb air pollution gases.

Seoul National University used to have a dozen campuses in Seoul. President Park arranged a new main campus in 1971. He ordered to construct a beautiful campus based on an ecological design of maintaining both natural topography and views. He directed application of the theory of landscape design introduced first in Ian McHarg's (1920-2001) book, *"Design with Nature'"* (1969), which was unfamiliar at that time in Korea.

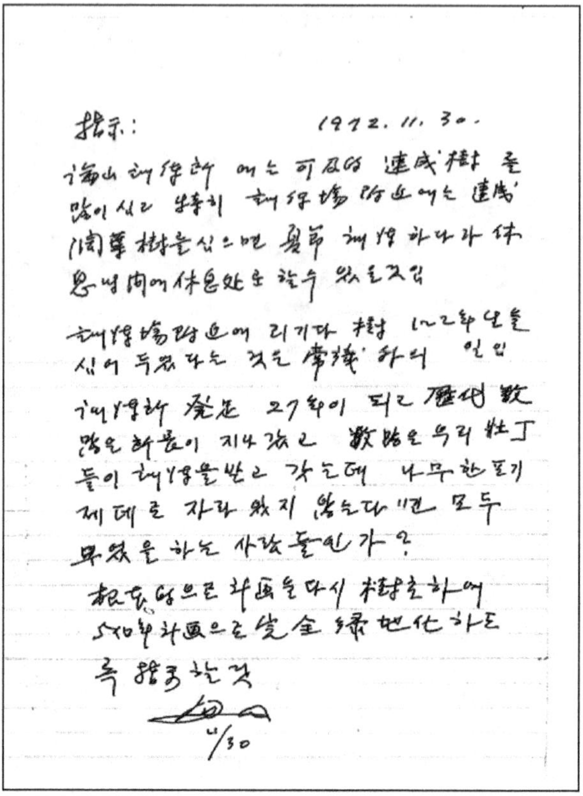

指示: 1972. 11. 30.

論山訓練所에는 可及的 速成樹를 많이 심고 특히 訓練場 周邊에는 速成闊葉樹를 심으면 夏節 訓練하다가 休息時間에 休息處로 할수 있도록 할것

訓練場 周邊에 리기다 松 1~2年生을 심어 두었다는 것은 常識 以外의 일임

訓練所 發足 27年이 되고 歷代 數많은 所長들이 지나갔고 數百萬 우리 壯丁들이 訓練을 받고 갔는데 나무 한포기 제대로 자라지 않는다니 모두 무엇을 하는 사람들인가?

根本的으로 計劃을 다시 樹立하여 5個年 計劃으로 完全 綠地化하도록 指導할것

11/30

Photo 87. President Park's own handwriting showing his deep interest in making even an inch more green zone and shade for the training soldiers in the Nonsan recruit training center (November 30, 1972)

In 1972, around the time when Oh Whee-Young was appointed as secretary for landscaping, landscaping experts filled the Blue House, one after another. President Park had such interest in landscaping that he issued two or three items of relevant instruction a month to secretary Oh. Among them, an instruction on Nonsan Soldier Training Center remains in President Park's own handwriting.

> "In Nonsan Training Center, plant fast-growing trees, as many as possible, and especially, fast-growing broadleaved trees in the vicinity of the drill field so that they may be used for a resting place during the summer training. It is beyond understanding that one- or two-year-old pitch pine trees have been planted in the vicinity of the drill field. Considering that it has been twenty-seven years since the numerous directors as well as our trainee soldiers stayed

at the training center, what are these people doing when there is no tree or grass growing? Reestablish the plan basically for a complete landscaping with a five-year plan. November 30, 1972, Park Chung-Hee."[12]

President Park's keen interest in landscaping was shown in numerous occasions. First of all, let's hear what secretary Oh Whee-Young says:

"It was one Saturday afternoon in July 1972. After finishing work, I received a notice to re-enter promptly because President Park was about to visit Asan Hyeonchungsa Shrine. At this time, though construction work at Hyeonchungsa was in considerable progress, its landscaping had just started. Without sufficient time in advance for review, when I checked on the site with the president, the following things were indicated: 1) The parking lot was too close to the front gate, disturbing the pious atmosphere. 2) The surrounding area being old rice paddies had a drainage problem. 3) Donated big trees for transplant arrived with improper root pruning."

Remedial measures by the president included the following: 1) Make an artificial hillock between the parking lot and ramp and set up a forest belt for a pious atmosphere. 2) For the sake of drainage, make a pond, raise the earth around, and plant trees on it. 3) Plant many indigenous fruit-bearing trees to attract birds.

Even after the completion of the construction work, President Park frequented there and gave many instructions. They included breeding carp in the pond, keeping students from chewing gum within the precincts of the shrine, using preservative treatments on the Chungmugong's old wooden houses. The comprehensive landscaping construction was performed from 1972 through 1974, planting a total of 96,274 trees.

The President's View of Landscaping

President Park usually favored native woody species, but it seems that he did not always emphasize indigenous trees for landscaping. He prized the Japanese umbrella pine (*Sciadopitys verticillata*) indigenous to Japan, dedicating it in December 1970 to the ancestral shrine of Hyeonchungsa and Dosan Seowon, founded by the great scholar Lee Toe-Gye. His planting of Japanese umbrella pine, traditionally deified by the Japanese, before the shrine in worship of Admiral Lee Sun-Shin still rouses controversy. But it is now the age of internationalization. Regardless of the place of origin or worship by a specific nation, more and more people plant beautiful trees with an open mind. The Japanese flowering cherry, called Sakura by the Japanese, is regarded as their national flower. On the Potomac River of Washington, DC, USA, lined cherry trees present a grand sight. During the Second World War with Japan, these cherry trees did not become the object of controversy in the United States. In Korea, cherry blossom festivals are popular among people, all of which are considered an example to of an open mind.

Professor Pae Jeong-Hann, Seoul National University, says: [14]

> "Park Chung-Hee's interest in landscaping is certainly above an amateurish practice of a hobby. At a quasi-landscape architect level, he planned and proceeded with landscaping projects. Through the comprehensive education of the Daegu School of Education, he had a considerable knowledge of art and plants, understood accurately the physical aspect of a mountain according to contour lines in designing the Seoul-Busan Expressway as a former army artillery officer skilled at map reading, and applied this in setting up a landscaping plan, too."

According to his aide Kim Chung-Yum, presidential Chief of Staff, President Park would think of himself as a first-class landscape architect:

> "It was frequent that President Park, even after work, was immersed in devising, writing memos, and drawing, and he issued orders the next morning. For example, he proposed, in person, methods of developing hillocks, how to fell trees for new planting, improvements on the farm village structure, landscaping around highways, points for installing rest areas, and concrete points of remodeling tour complexes "[15]

Though not undertaking professional lessons on landscaping, President Park, in the opinion of experts, was equipped with professional expertise. Anyway, about landscaping, President Park's venture was quite expansive. The Yeocheon petrochemical complex is a comprehensive complex on the world's largest scale with a three million-ton level of ethylene output. A large wharf was constructed so that 100,000 ton-level cargo ships might be able to dock, which President Park visited many times. He ordered full-scale landscaping, stressing that the area also needed the world's top-level cleaning and beautification since it was the place often visited by foreign sailors. This occasion provided an opportunity to hold a national contest for the best industrial complex for commendation. It was a contest for judging landscaping, beautification, and tidiness comprehensively. [18]

On December 17, 1976, Park Geun-Hye, the President Park's elder daughter who became the eighteenth president in 2013, said in an interview with KBS, "Several days ago I hung a new calendar containing pictures of Europe's rich farm village scenery. Then my father came in, so I said, 'Can't our farm village become rich like this?' and he said confidently, 'It won't be long before we become that way."[16] This comment suggests that Park Chung-Hee's picture of the future farm village was idyllic and nostalgic like those in Europe.

President Park's will toward making the farm village's scenery beautiful this way is confirmed by Kim Du-Yeong (Former Blue House secretary).[27] In 1979, Vice Premier Shin Hyeon-Hwak proposed reducing the budget for the farm village structure improvement project as he drafted a curtailed budget due to the global oil crisis. President Park said, "Let it be that way." On the proposal again later, he rejected it again saying, "This is my life's work....." So Vice Premier Shin proposed a third time and finally accomplished his proposals for budget cuts.

Cultural Assets Landscaping

The author already described that President Park started to protect the cultural properties almost discarded in the time of the Rhee Syng-Man government by enacting the "Cultural Treasure Protection Law" in 1962 right after the revolution. From an early age, he showed a special interest in restoration of historical sites, personally taking good care of the landscaping of historical sites. On August 29, 1968, President Park showed a sincere interest in the landscaping of the Hyeonchungsa Shrine as described earlier, saying, "Sanctification of Hyeonchungsa has a larger ethnic meaning than building scores or hundreds of factories.

To enhance our people's spirit of defending our fatherland, we will purify our ancestors' historical sites around the country and sanctify them into holy precincts."[20)

In 1974, by establishing a Five-Year Literature Restoration Plan, he focused on enforcing the conservation, repairs, and cleanup projects for the remains of country-defending warriors and great men. He also established the secondary Five-Year Literature Restoration Plan in 1978. This project included the translation of classics into modern Korean, creation of the Academy of Korean Studies, and the conservation of the King Sejong Tomb, and Andong Dosanseowon. [12)

Photo 88. President Park hurried in restoring cultural assets damaged and left alone from the start of his coming into power, achieving restoration of the Bulguksa Temple built during the Shilla Dynasty. Trees in the background are Korean red pines, beloved most by the Korean people (a photo courtesy of Oh Whee-Young).

On July 3, 1973 he issued an order to plant trees at the opening ceremony for restoring Bulguksa Temple, the most beloved temple in this country. It was to beautify the back side of toilets for Bulguksa parking lot by planting cherry trees and to remove scrubs growing wild on Namsan behind the House of Hwarang (Shilla Chivalry) by substituting suitable tree species. It is said that people wondered why the president had to interfere in tree-planting around the toilet. It was certainly because of his particular love of trees and nature. While going around the countryside by car, he looked out the window and often said to his entourage, "There used to be a good zelkova tree there. Who felled it?" Thinking that Korea's fields and mountains were his gardens, he didn't carelessly go past one tree or one grass, recorded Jo Gap-Je. [5]

Here is one episode. One day, President Park asked Choi Gak-Gyu, Minister of the Economic Planning Board, "Will you give me 10 billion won (US $20.6 million)?" The minister asked, "What for, President?" The president answered, "I want to use it for landscaping historical sites." With some discontent, Minister Choi would grumble to other cabinet members, "The president, it seems, is going to landscape all the country."

The author would comment on President Park's view of landscaping as follow. From the beginning of his regime, President Park attached importance to our people's culture and traditions. As a developing country imitates Western society materially, it naturally increases a desire for traditional culture. It seems that President Park emphasized nationalism-based tradition in his landscaping too. While making the desolate mountains and forests green, he intended to improve the environment of cities and farm villages and to build a beautiful rural community through landscaping.

While Park Chung-Hee emphasized Korean-style landscaping, he also received the criticism of sticking to the Japanese style, such as Chinese juniper and rock masonry favored by the Japanese people. In particular, President Park was also reprimanded as pro-Japanese because he liked the Japanese umbrella pine (*Sciadopitys verticillata*) esteemed by the Japanese people.

At the beginning of the 1970s, our people's national income was rising up from $300 to $500. It was also the time that Kim Hyun-Ok, Seoul mayor, was building low-priced apartment houses in an effort to introduce an apartment culture in a crowded Seoul city. At that time when the value of our lives felt so small, President Park was preparing feast for our eyes.

Maintenance of Landscape Trees at the Blue House

Speaking of landscaping, we cannot leave out the topic about gardening at the Blue House. The following is a story by Park Weon-Geun. Park worked as a gardener for the Blue House from 1969 until 1979, aiding President Park in gardening. The Blue House was on the same site of the old government-general residence under Japanese imperialism, and previously there was a Buddhist temple inside. Many old trees were conserved, including large fir trees. For the sake of convenience, the content of this discussion will be presented by numbering each topic.

1. President's branch pruning in person: If he had time after lunch, the president pruned the branches of garden trees in person with the gardener. He enjoyed pruning by climbing up a ladder. He always had pruning shears in a drawer in his office. After his assassination in October 1979, a variety of pruning shears was found from his drawers.

2. Trees favored by the president: He liked cherry, magnolia, and nut trees, among tree species in the precincts. He asked to plant many common apricot, persimmon, and chestnut trees. Like First Lady Yook Young-Soo, he liked magnolias and there were many magnolias in the precincts. A poem he wrote at the beginning of marriage survives in which he compared his wife to a magnolia.

Photo 89. In landscaping the precincts of the Blue House, magnolias would be likened to first lady Yook Young-Soo (Spring 1971)

3. Himalayan cedar: It was one of the president's favorite trees. Particularly, in Daegu, he had been planting it for a long time because the weather of there was quite mild in winter. Himalayan cedars planted at Dongdaegu station as a roadside tree were also the result of President Park's order, which are even now growing splendidly as big trees.

4. Common apricot: There were many common apricots in the precincts. Saying it would help the farm-house income, the president collected and sent the seeds to the Forest Service with an order to cultivate the seedlings and spread them to farm houses.

5. Direction of measures about damage by asphalt: There were many old trees in the precincts, and after noticing dying branches on the side of asphalt cover, the president asked the gardener to take measures. A hole was bored in the asphalt to allow air to get to the roots, and a pail was installed to let water flow in bit by bit.

Photo 90. President Park planted many fruit trees in the Blue House and encouraged the farmers to plant them for food. In the autumn he enjoyed picking up a part of the fruits and left other parts for wild animals.

6. Construction of a glasshouse: As soon as Park Weon-Geun started work in 1969, he was allowed to build a glasshouse in the Blue House. From this glasshouse, plants given as gifts and flowerpots for interior decoration needed in the precincts were cultivated, and later fresh vegetables (lettuce, young radishes, paprika) were grown on a small scale to bring them on the president's dining table.

7. Interior plant decoration: There were a few flower-pots in every room in the president's office. It was the responsibility of the gardener to exchange the flower-pots in the offices. The president liked flowers with scent, orchids, royal azaleas and Japanese azaleas. To decorate with flowers, cut flowers were purchased from Namdaemun (South Gate) Market a couple of times a week. When a foreign visitor came into the Blue House, the gardener tried to decorate the reception room with plants or flowers originating from the visitor's country. By putting a memo of plant names under the table, the gardener tried to make an environment for smooth conversation between the leaders.

8. Do not sweep leaf litter: Even when there was leaf litter in the autumn, the president ordered that fallen leaves on the promenade be left alone. It was to enable one to enjoy the mood of the autumn as long as possible.

9. Consideration for plants and wild animals: At that time, in the yard of the Blue House, persimmon and chestnut trees were planted too. One year, seeing too many persimmons hanging on some weak branches, President Park picked them evenly and smiled saying, "Now the branches will have less difficulty."[2] There was a considerable number of fruit-bearing trees in the precincts. Some of the fruits were harvested but an order was given to leave the fruits of the persimmon, chestnut, and acorn-producing oaks. It was in consideration to provide foods for mountain birds, squirrels, and wild animals in the precincts.

10. Commemorative tree-planting and the reality of failing to preserve history: On Arbor Day, trees were often planted to commemorate this day in the precincts too. Commemorative plantings included unusual trees such as the golden rain-tree or mountain ash. After tree-planting, a wooden or stone post was installed with a name of the president. It was surmised that earlier, Presidents Rhee Syng-Man and Yoon Bo-Seon also might have planted trees to commemorate this day. However, there were no posts or inscriptions with their names found in the

precincts. President Park felt sorry for the political reality that couldn't preserve history as it was. The author recently checked trees planted for commemoration with an inscription in the precincts and found that only one tree of Chinese juniper planted by President Park in 1978 remained with a stone inscription. After that, trees planted by successive presidents have been properly preserved with inscriptions.

Photo 91. Of trees planted in the Blue House by President Park, there is only one Chinese juniper left with a marker stone planted in 1978. Trees planted earlier by former presidents for commemoration have no traces left.

Bare Hills Landscaping in Daegwallyeong

Now the topic is on special landscape planting, which is different from general tree planting of digging a simple hole. This story took place in the neighborhood of the Daegwallyeong rest stop on the old Yeongdong Expressway. It is known as a place for people going to Gangneung and arriving at Daegwallyeong to enjoy some fresh air. It had extensive clumsy bushes in the vicinity of the summit of Daegwallyeong at 850 m above sea level. It is an area with 30 m/s strong winds blowing incessantly all year round and with bitter winter cold and over 2 m accumulation of snow. Nearly every tree planted failed to take root except the eulalia grass and low bushes growing naturally.

In the 1960s, in Gangwon-do, slash-and-burn farmers were damaging the mountain forests here and there on a large scale. In 1967, the Gangwon-do provincial government cleared 168 ha of hill-area forest in Daegwanllyeong and invited the farmers to settle down together for farming. Because of the poor climatic condition of this region, however, farmers failed to continue farming, leaving an extensive barren land instead.

As the Yeongdong Expressway was completed in 1975, President Park asked Sohn Soo-Ik, Head of the Forest Service to create a special tree planting. After successive research and meetings, the Forest Service decided to adopt "special landscape planting". The work started in the spring of 1976 as soon as the ground thawed. First, terraces were made as in the erosion-control work to prevent the washing down of soil on slopes. Then, to align in any direction seen from the road, large seedlings (1 m in height) of Korean white pine, larch, fir, Norway spruce, birch, and alder with strong cold hardiness were planted. A triangular support and a circular blind made of sasa were put up around each tree. In addition, for the whole area, wooden fences 3 m in height and 20 m in length were installed in a total of 4.8 km to block the wind.

Photo 92. Sohn Soo-Ik (center with both hands folding back), Head of the Forest Service, is checking a round protection bamboo blind installed for each tree at the Daegwallyeong special landscape planting at 850m above sea level in a severe strong wind.

Photo 93. Daegwallyeong special landscape planting was a unique case in which large trees were planted with wind fences surrounded to protect them.

The biggest construction work was brought-in soil. Due to the very poor soil, planting trees required soil rich in nutrients to be brought in from another place. Rice paddy soil was carried from Hoenggye in Gangwon-do with dump trucks. While the truck drove the ascent of Daegwallyeong, meanderingly spouting blackish exhaust fumes, laborers climbed up toward the summit, making a long line with their coolie racks filled with soil. Seen from a helicopter, it would have looked like ants carrying their food. Staff of the regional forest office and laborers at work poured in meager but sincere efforts, lodging together in the mountain during the period of work. During the first year of 1976, they planted 45,000 trees in 17 ha, and the planting continued each year until 1986. In eleven years of desperate efforts, they planted a total of 843,000 large seedlings in 311 ha. Since completion of the work, Daegwallyeong has been widely known, and to this day, as a model plantation that established a beautiful forest by overcoming the limitations of nature.

Photo 94. Daegwallyeong's special landscape planting established overcoming the poor environment in the latter half of the 1970s is famous as a site receiving unstinted praise from forest specialists. Even foreign scientists who attended Seoul IUFRO (International Union of Forestry Research Organization) in August 2010 inspected this place and gave a cry of wonder.

Chapter 18. Care for Trees and Nature Conservation

Designation of Tree Care Day and Development of Forest Fertilizer

Planting trees in spring and leaving them alone through summer often makes trees fail to grow properly. Watering during periods of drought and fertilizing help trees grow more healthily. However, it is not easy to revisit and care for trees on distant mountains. It seems that President Park had an unusual love for trees. Sohn Soo-Ik, Head of Forest Service, recalls the president asking: [11)]

> "Why don't we have tree care day when we have Arbor Day? What about setting a tree care day in the fall to fertilize, prune, and remove miscellaneous trees? Isn't it a way to help spring-planted trees grow better?"

This idea gave birth to Tree Care Day in 1977, which was set as the first Saturday of November each year to avoid conflict with the busy farming season. At this event, President Park attended in person, while all officials participated by region and institution. They revisited the planting sites to check how well the trees were thriving. They removed grass and encouraged growth by fertilizing trees. This activity deepened interest in forest conservation, which grew into a nature conservation movement later.

Sohn records the event like this: "In fact, for trees, tending care is no less important than planting. That is why from ancient times, there is a saying that 'A tree planted in a mountain grows at the footstep of the mountain owner.' According to the Ten-Year Forest Rehabilitation Plan, the Forest Service was doing a thorough post-planting inspection for survival of every tree planted in the spring. In addition, President Park's designation of Tree care Day promoted additional encouragement for the forestry officials." [11]

President Park had such an interest in tree care that he gave instructions to develop forest fertilizer and came up with new ideas himself. He said that trees planted on a mountain would grow better if fertilizer was given. He feared sending out general fertilizer to a farm village, however, because farmers might use it for farming instead of for the trees. Thus, the president instructed the secretariat on July 6, 1976, to develop fertilizer for tree-use only, testified Kim Chung-Yum, chief secretary. [9] He even set a standard that forest fertilizer should be melted out slowly and be easy to be carried in rugged mountain. This finally gave birth to a molded forest compound fertilizer. It was made hard by mixing with clay and looked like a peach pit. Forest fertilizer was manufactured by private companies, but purchased by the government in the whole quantity and distributed to every village for free. It was not suited for general farming because the fertilizer ingredients melted out slowly for over two years, records Kim Yeon-Pyo [21].

Photo 95. President Park ordered the manufacture of a fertilizer exclusively for forest use. It was devised with a thick clay ball with nutrients melting out slowly in order not to be used for farming.

President Park was special in that he was both a "man of honor" who took care of a tree once planted and a "gentleman of consideration" who gave careful attention so that farmers would not be led to dishonest use of the free fertilizer. President Park attended the event of Tree Care Day two times until his death in 1979. However, the Tree Care Day event continued until the latter part of the 1990s.

Spearheading the Nature Conservation Movement

President Park was also the one who first advocated nature conservation. In the middle of the 1970s, as per capita national income rose over $800, with the opening of the highway, sightseeing and recreation started to boom. Holiday makers crowding mountains and valleys began to trample the countryside. Air and water pollution also followed because of industrial development.

On September 5, 1977, President Park had an opportunity to visit his birthplace during provincial inspections. Arriving at the provincial park of Mt. Geumo, Gyeongbuk, he came up to the summit by cable car and watched a nearby cascade. He was able to see distinctly Sangmo-dong on the skirt of Mt. Geumo where he was born and Gumi Elementary School, which he had attended, which must have filled his heart with emotion. But then there was an eyesore for him. He found in the stream residue of rice, packing paper, cans, and empty bottles thrown away at random. Instead of chiding relevant officials, he proposed cleaning to all and took the lead in picking up garbage for over thirty minutes. President Park climbed down on foot without taking the cable car. His heart filled with emotion of old memories must have been disturbed. Climbing down along the trail, he also picked up a large amount of garbage.

On September 10, five days later, President Park advocated a nature conservation movement at the Monthly Meetings on Economic Trends because he had experienced such a shock from Mt. Geumo. The result of the meeting was the decision to organize a nature conservation committee headed by the Prime Minister, nature conservation council composed of twenty-one civilians, and 44,000 nature conservation societies around the country. About two months after the resolution to set up an organ for nature conservation, November 5, 1977, was the first Tree Care Day. On this day, the government held a Nature Conservation National Rally. It was a bugle to spread a state-level nature conservation campaign. Like this, tree care and nature conservation have different names but the same root.

Photo 96. President Park (one with a cane), who came out for the nature conservation movement at Mt. Bukhan National Park, Seoul. He was a leader who was familiar with the symbolism of his behavior.

At a new-year press conference on January 18, 1978, he clarified his views on nature and forests. An address at a new-year press conference is a presentation of administrative policy for the coming year, that is, an enforcement ordinances. He said,

> "Nature is our living environment……. I believe that only when dense forest, which is a source of clean rivers and atmosphere, is beautifully harmonized with a highly industrialized society can we enjoy a rich life in a healthy and dignified spiritual culture."

President Park didn't stop at this address, but put the enforcement ordinance into practice in person. Finishing the half-a-day's work on Saturday, he and the Blue House personnel came out with a broom in the afternoon to clean the nearby road. President Park's company also did nature conservation campaigning, such as picking up garbage at Mt. Bukhan valley. On November 14, 1978 President Park spent his last birthday silently at Mt. Seolak with his two daughters. He picked up garbage as he climbed up Biseondae. Such acts by the president made holiday makers not want to leave the smallest rubbish, while middle and high school students came out to the banks of the Han River to clean up the area.

Marking the first anniversary of the nature conservation movement on October 5, 1978, the government held a ceremony to declare a Nature Conservation Chapter. In particular, 1978 was the year that the government accomplished the Ten-Year Forest Rehabilitation Plan in just six years' time. This year, mountains around the country began to become denser, bringing about our people's self-confidence and forming the necessity for nature conservation.

The Nature Conservation Chapter was enacted with help from the nature conservation movement spreading globally. This emphasizes each person's sincere practice with an aim to cherish nature and hand down precious natural resources for good to offspring. Since that time, nature conservation has become part of our culture. It is a good thing that income and living standards have risen, followed by the proportional high awareness of nature conservation.

Photo 97. President Park took the lead in the nature conservation movement by cleaning the front yard of the Blue House.

Personnel Matters Like Planting a Tree

So far we have looked into President Park's loyalty or consideration in relation to trees or nature. So what was his loyalty or consideration about his men? President Park prized competent and devoted elite bureaucrats very much. Unless a particular reason occurred, he allowed them to remain in their posts for a long time because he knew it was the best way to secure the consistency of policies and stabilization of the national administration. Nam Deok-Woo, Seogang University professor of economics, worked with President Park for ten years from 1969. His thoughts are recorded by Kim In-Man as follows:

> "This is the analysis by professional institutions including the World Bank and economists abroad. Park Chung-Hee induced elite officials to be devoted to national development with an amazing passion. He did not subjugate high officials with power but treated them as partners in creating national interests, encouraging and putting them up forward. At times, he took care of them with horizontal humane sympathy, not a hierarchy. He allowed persons with recognized capability to work together for an extended period. The president's confidence was the very motivating power that moved elite officials."[2]

Goh Kun, a former prime minister, recalls, "At that time, looking at the picture of our desolate country turning green, we were energetic even without eating or sleep." It was because President Park decided on the right course and induced a sense of mission and pride among the officials with his strong confidence and continuous encouragement.

President Park appointed only persons who had been thoroughly "tested". Kim Chung-Yum, former presidential Chief of Staff, said that the president's first tour of inspection or every meeting such as an export promotion meeting was used for the purpose of testing the officials' capability. In addition, it was said that President Park entrusted the ministers with the task of appointing personnel of vice minister and under. Doing so was both to show his confidence in the ministers and to create an environment in which a minister could perform his duties to his heart's content.

President Park attached importance to the site and the person in charge. It was probably the product of his overseeing administration. On

April 17, 1975, President Park inspected the site of the Yeongil erosion-control project. Because of the strong rain and wind that hindered his helicopter from taking off, Park's company rode in a jeep, struggling along the unpaved hard pass of only three meter's width to the site. The purpose of the trip was to encourage the employees at the site in person. Bae Jin Seong left a record as follows:

> "The briefing chart board had to be held by two people together, and its paper was blown off, torn by the storm. The president's visit to the site in this bad weather lifted the employees' spirits to the sky."[22]

Photo 98. President Park (left) was never absent from the Arbor Day events while listening to the opinions of Dr. Hyun Shin-Kyu (center), a world-famous forest geneticist.

President Park not only thought much of incumbent persons but also listened to specialists who had different opinions. In late spring of 1973, on one Saturday afternoon, presidential Chief of Staff Kim Chung-Yum visited the Institute of Forest Genetics in Suwon. He was sent by President Park to hear the opinion of Dr. Hyun Shin-Kyu, senior professor at Seoul National University and founder of this institute, on the forest rehabilitation plan. Dr. Hyun pointed out to Chief of Staff Kim problems of forest rehabilitation being pushed forward impatiently. Considering that numerous trees planted in the past mostly failed to survive, he proposed that the reforestation project be performed step by step based on the objective and scientific evaluation of the causes. Though it was the opposite opinion of President Park's principle of "early achievement" of reforestation, the president accepted Dr. Hyun's proposal and allowed the organization of an evaluation team composed of forestry professors.

Dr. Hyun had improved the Italian poplar and developed the pitch-lolly pine and *Populusalba* x *glandulosa*. President Park treated him politely as a senior scholar, mentioning many times planting as many *Populusalba* x *glandulosa* as possible at every Arbor Day event. President Park enjoyed meeting Dr. Hyun at every annual event of Arbor Day. When it was nearing Arbor Day, he told his secretaries to check in advance if Dr. Hyun was going to attend the Arbor Day event. On May 16, 1978 President Park conferred the "May 16 People's Award" on Dr. Hyun, where he presented the "Hyun poplar", a new name for *Populusalba* x *glandulosa*, taking the surname of Dr. Hyun. On Tree Care Day of that year, the president also gave a jeep to Dr. Hyun. [23]

Jo gap-Je summarized President Park's method of ruling the country like this: [5]

> As a genius at system operations, Park Chung-Hee 1) set up the most important goals numerically, 2) clarified the roles of each institution for achieving these goals, 3) had personnel policy of the right man in the right place, 4) concentrated the capability of each man on this direction, 5) confirmed and checked the process of execution institutionally, and 6) repeated revision and encouragement in his national administration.

The author agrees with Jo. The president's success in the reforestation project is thought to be due to 1) definite goal as a national policy project, 2) personnel policy of appointing the capable man, 3) establishment of circumstances in which staff can exercise their capabilities, and 4) thorough check and superintendence.

In other words, President Park used men as he planted and grew trees. As he decided on ten major tree species urgent for reforestation, he appointed tested men to important posts, regardless of familiarity or their home-town. As after planting he focused on tree care such as fertilizing, he allowed a person already appointed to exercise his capability to the full. As he cried for nature conservation to save planted trees and mountains, he protected and encouraged his men and operated a system properly to achieve the goal.

Chapter 19. Beat a Drum of Victory

Credit of Aerial Photography

In establishing a tree-planting plan, the most decisive data came through aerial photography. The reforestation area data could be collected by the guesswork of the Ri-Dong village forest cooperative staff or Gun forest section officials, but that method was literally outdated. It was most reasonable to base data on aerial photography when we try to set priorities of tree-planting or erosion-control projects. Aerial photography is essential for tree care or other management. Hence the first credit goes to aerial photography in maximizing the result of the forest rehabilitation project.

Aerial photographs of Korea's forests were first made by the "UN Korea Forest Survey Institute" in 1964, prepared by UN special funds. [1] The institute photographed the Nakdong River basin in 1967 and finished the first forest survey during the period from 1968 to 1970. Fortunately, based on this, urgent erosion-control projects on the three river basins (Han River, Nakdong River, and Geum River) were finished in 1971 and 1972.

In January 1974, Sohn Soo-Ik, Head of the Forest Service, gathered executives of the Forest Service together. It was about one year after his appointment. He said that in order to proceed with planting trees in accordance with Ten-Year Forest Rehabilitation Plan without a hitch, it was the top priority to know the result of tree-planting projects enforced over the past ten years. All executives agreed. To determine this, the conclusion was reached that it was most efficient to take aerial photos and analyze them. It was not knowledge but money that mattered now.

Photo 99. The initial picture of winning the war against bare mountains. The mountain still exposing its skeleton, with green clothes that cover the mountain softly looks beautiful (Reforestation success region, Pocheon-gun, Gyeonggi-do).

Sohn issued a strict order to finish the photographing of 5.76 million ha of the whole country (then, the forest area of the country was 6.64 million ha) before the end of that year, even by winning a special budget. Executives of the Forest Service first tried to prepare finances by diverting their own budgets, but money was in short supply. Insufficient finances must be covered by a reserve fund. Though diverting budgets was possible with the approval of the Economic Planning Board, a reserve fund was a matter that required approval by the president. It was in July that, after vicissitudes, permitting a reserve fund was obtained.

Korea's weather is not suitable for taking aerial photographs. Aerial photography requires continuously clear weather without a cloud. But, by thirty years' average, clear days in our country are only thirty-one days in a year, and around 50 percent of these are in September and October. Fortunately in 1974, there were unexpectedly many clear days in May, June, August, and September. This made trees planted in the spring dry out easily but allowed photographing successfully as planned. It was a great fortune that based on this, the forest rehabilitation project hit its stride after all.

Photo 100. As a gleam of success in the forest reclamation appeared, the government issued a commemorative stamp for the national tree planting period to add fresh fuel to the project (March 20, 1975).

Anecdote of Arbor Day and Small Misjudgment

Earlier, the author said that President Park never failed to attend the Arbor Day event. At the president's initiative, public institutions around the country dealt with the tree-planting event in a significant way. The Forest Service dispatched its personnel to tree-planting events of the institutions around the country to supervise so that its tree-planting event might be properly executed, and whether the Head attended or not was one of the major report items.

After returning from the United States, the author, working at the Institute of Forest Genetics under the Forest Service, attended the government agency's planting event as a supervisor in 1980 for the first time. It is remembered as a tree-planting event of the Ministry of Communications held in Yongin-gun, Gyeonggi-do, and over a hundred people, including the minister and bureau heads planted white pines all morning. It was an opportunity for the author to experience the actual scene of domestic reforestation heretofore unseen for the past eight years while studying abroad. And the picture of diligent shoveling, even by women staffers rolling up their sleeves, still remains as a touching memory.

President Park said at the Arbor Day event held in Yongin-gun, Gyeonggido in 1972, "Some responsibility of our country's destruction of mountain forests lies with the military units. It is true that in the past, civilians and soldiers felled trees recklessly using army trucks for securing fuel wood or the unit members' welfare. We did so when I was engaged as an army unit chief in the region of Gangwon-do. So army units, feeling the responsibility to take the lead in tree-planting of the country, should be active in this matter."

Truly, President Park used woods by illegal cutting in his army days, but when he rose to the First Army chief of staff as major general, he was the one who eradicated the "welfare business" and the use of firewood in the First Army. Even after curing the two maladies, he seemed to have a considerable burden in his mind and endeavored to pay off the debts. The author wishes the politicians in our country would also be armed with this kind of spirit.

There is another episode related to Arbor Day.[1] The forest in the Forest Experiment Station, Gwangneung, Gyeonggi-do, was preserved well by the staff's devoted endeavors, even during the Korean War. With a beautiful natural forest unmatched by any other places in the country, this is the place where President Park had many tree-planting events. On Arbor Day of one year, during the lunch break, a wild rabbit appeared nearby. President Park stopped eating and ran after the rabbit. Of course, he failed to catch it, but his instantaneous childlike innocence was nothing different from any person. Many people having lunch together, as well as his bodyguards, were at their wits' end for a while. Feeling satisfied with a better environment of dense forest with rabbits inhabiting it, he must have returned to his childlike innocence momentarily.

There is a second episode. While moving for two and a half hours from Suwon to the Daegu Interchange for inspection of Gyeongbuk in February 1976, President Park issued in the car a total of forty-eight directives about the mountain forest along the highway. It means that he gave a directive every three minutes and every 4 km in terms of time and distance. Kim Yeon-Pyo, the tree-planting section chief, recorded all these instructions. Later, it took three days for Sohn, Head of the Forest Service, to check on the site with Kim. The president's grasp of problems were acute, and his methods of restoration and instructions on the cut slope were very concrete. [21]

Photo 101. Chupungryeong-style reforestation ordered by President Park received a comment that it was not suited for regular tree planting due to too large of a planting space except for the chestnut trees (Chestnut complex in Pocheon-gun, Gyeonggi-do).

Of course, it is not true that President Park issued correct instructions all the time. His instructions sometimes included content that turned out to be unsuccessful. One example is a story about the Douglas-fir. In the 1970s, there was an ambassador to the United States who was captivated by the Douglas-fir that grew up straight in the western region, making a dense forest. Through the channel of the Ministry of Foreign Affairs, the ambassador sent 100,000 seedlings to the Institute of Forest Genetics by air, appending the president's special instructions. The institute had a great difficulty in overwintering this many plants. The next year, the institute tried to plant the seedlings across the country, but all failed because the Korean climate was not suitable for Douglas-fir.

Planting Trees with a Loan from the World Bank

In 1976, there was a special project of establishing the fuel-wood forest with a loan from the World Bank.[1] In the spring of 1975, the Economic Planning Board, applauding the fuel-wood forest project driven by the Forest Service so far, suggested applying for an IBRD loan. Upon this opportunity, $4.16 million of "Saemaul project loan" was obtained in 1976 to 1977 to establish a fuel-wood forest. It was globally unprecedented that a fund loan was invested in a reforestation project.

The government, aiming to make a total 207,000 ha of fuel-wood forest for the First Ten-Year Forest Rehabilitation Plan, established a 127,000 ha fuel-wood forest from 1976 until 1977 with the World Bank loan. In addition, instead of motorcycle-level means of field transportation, a Japanese-made Toyota small truck was distributed to each city and Gun with the fund loan, which lifted the spirits of front forest officials very much. The $1.42 million (annual interest 8.5 percent) and $2.74 million (annual interest 4.5 percent) loans were introduced on the condition of a twenty-five-year redemption, including a term of seven years of the loan. If the fuel-wood forest project and reforestation project ended in failure, it would mean a waste of dear loan money. Thus this project wouldn't have started without the government's strong will toward reforestation and its thorough oversight. In 2000, the principal was all redeemed.

Photo 102. Pitch-lolly hybrid pine makes a good stand with straight stems and fast growth, combining the desirable characteristics of both parents. This pine was planted in the southern part of Korea with mild winter.

When the reforestation project was mobilizing and a fund loan was in the middle of being procured, a US broadcasting company, CBS obtained information about the Korea's World Bank loan and attempted to discover whether the money was actually being properly used for reforestation or whether there was government-level irrationality. In the spring of 1977, a CBS news team came to Korea and investigated the project while traveling around the country. Closely covering the sites of the fuel-wood forest establishment and erosion-control project, the reporters soon realized that their thoughts had been wrong from the start. They examined written planting records, witnessed farm village residents planting trees assiduously as a part of the "Saemaul Movement", and saw forest officials devotedly sweating in their thorough guidance and supervision. Naturally, they were convinced that it would become a very successful reforestation to touch the world rather than to find irrationality.

In addition, they became aware that in some part of the reforestation, farm village residents attended in the form of "forced labor" without wages to establish fuel-wood forest. The Temporary Act of Forest Reclamation enacted early in 1963 allowed forced labor of farm residents, if necessary, and enabled the government to mobilize Village Forestry Cooperative members for forced labor in accordance with the Act of National Reconstruction Movement. They came to know that many benefits, including gathering fuel wood, were given to those who performed forced labor faithfully. Finally, CBS came to report Korea's reforestation and national reconstruction projects very affirmatively. Praising the Koreans' patriotism and young people's cooperation and public spirit based on the Saemaul Movement it delivered a story on the high probability of success to the whole world.

After this report, the UN FAO (Food and Agriculture Organization) informed us that they would inspect Korea's site of forest rehabilitation, and in 1982 it published an FAO report titled "Village Forestry Development in the Republic of Korea" [33]. This report extolled "Korea as the only developing country since World War II that has succeeded in reforestation." Only after being informed that many South Asian countries would come for inspection, did the Forest Service realize that CBS had made an affirmative report. After that, there has been no end to the processions from many southeast countries to inspect Korea's successful Saemaul project and reforestation cases. [1]

There is an old saying, "God helps those who help themselves". We could not imagine these things. How could one predict that the World Bank would provide a loan for Korea's reforestation project and who would ever think that a US broadcasting company would publicize the story of Korea's struggle for reforestation to the whole world? However, it is the great lesson of our reforestation project that working one's head off will lead to victory in the battle and someday brings honor to ourselves.

Activity of Jeju-do Pony

In this battle, a story about riding on the back of pony cannot be left out.[1] For the management of plantations, frequent patrol of the forests is essential. In Germany there are many forest roads in the deepest forests that make it possible to patrol the mountains by car. In our country, however, there is nothing like a forest road but a trail such as in a fairy tale, which had been made by the footsteps of forest officials. That was the level of our reforestation and management.

The Forest Service hung patrol boxes at strategic points to have forest officials periodically sign their names. In the forest patrol, officers chiefly used motorcycles but when there was no mountain path, they had to walk in. It was so hard that there were people who quit the position of forest official.

Photo 103. In 1977, for inaccessible places without a forest road, officials inspected forests by riding a pony, showing a great struggle for forest reclamation.

At this time, Kim Yeong-Dal at the Forest Service came up with the idea of patrolling on a horse. He had been in Germany to study and saw in Spain that forest officials patrolled the forest on horseback. After proposing the idea to the Head of Forest Service, officials had twenty Jeju-do ponies trained in the army cavalry unit and then assigned them to the Chuncheon Regional Forest Office. They were not as large or imposing as a racing horse but very suitable for performing patrol duties while going around in the mountain.

Riding these ponies, it was possible to chase illegal cutters because in the mountain they were not able to outrun the horses. In addition, ponies earned good responses from residents and were given extensive coverage in the daily paper, which provided good publicity. As time went by, there arose a problem from inside. These ponies wouldn't run in the mountain. It turned out that the horse's hooves weren't cut properly, and being fed improperly, the horses had stomachaches. At last, because of unsuccessful management of the ponies this project was stopped after all. [1]

Six Major Factors of Success in Forest Reclamation

It is not an exaggeration that Sohn Soo-Ik, Head of the Forest Service, was a man born for the First Ten-Year Forest Rehabilitation Project. He served as the Head of the Forest Service for five years and eight months from January 16, 1973, until September 10, 1978. His record of holding office has not been broken yet. Sohn was the one who took responsibility for this project upon his appointment and left this position on its completion in six years much earlier than the target date.

During this period, Sohn broke the six hundred hours' record of helicopter riding. Especially between February 20 and May 14, 1978, Sohn taking along Kim Yeon-Pyo, tree-planting director, visited 109 village nurseries around the country, 87 plantations, and 23 erosion control sites. For 29 days, he visited a total of 219 places in person to check the actual condition of the sites. This was what Kim Yeon-Pyo said in his interview with the author, showing his old memo book in person.

A total of six hundred hours for six years is considered an air riding record that no high officials could possibly follow since the establishment of the government. His passion was such. While visiting the sites, Sohn carried about a stick with graduations in order to measure the size of seedlings, planting space, and planting angle in cutting. If not properly done, he was thorough enough to give a good scolding.[28] He has now become the legend of Korea's reforestation.

President Park showed a deep confidence in Sohn often expressing satisfaction with reforestation. He entrusted reforestation to Sohn, knowing Sohn's careful planning and sense of mission. Sohn, as Head of the Forest Service, led the forest reclamation with a thorough supervision of the sites and with guiding superintendence. The president might think that heaven assisted Sohn's enthusiasm by providing good fortune. In the latter half of the 1970s in the midst of reforestation, it rained often across the country in spring. One day the president shared conversation with Sohn like this:

"You are a lucky guy."
"What do you mean by that, President?"
"Each time you plant trees, it always rains, doesn't it?"

The president used some dialect from Gyeongbuk. While inspecting the site of reforestation with Sohn, he said,

"Look at that. There is a considerable Galbi piled up under the pine tree."

He was pleased with the leaf litter piles under the trees and with the mountain getting greener. "Galbi' is a Gyeongsang-do dialect word referring to dry pine leaves.

As the Forest Service possessed three helicopters for the first time in 1971, it founded the Forest Service Flying Corps. Until 1980 the service used seven helicopters for project of controlling harmful insects. In 1981, it began extinguishing forest fires using helicopters for the first time. Presently the Forest Service is equipped with fifty helicopters, which have become indispensable for extinguishing forest fires.

As the first forest rehabilitation plan was coming along with wind in its sail, President Park was looking another step farther, to establishing a commercial forest. He really seems to have been a person of excellent leadership and keen insight. In 1977, President Park repeated the following statement at a January new-year inspection of the Ministry of Home Affairs, at a February gubernatorial conference, and at a new-year inspection of Chungnam and Chungbuk.

Photo 104. Now dense forest has become familiar scenery that can be seen anywhere around the country with a very bright prospect for timber resources (forty-year-old Sugi forest at Jeju-do Hannam Experiment Forest)

"We should push ahead with the reforestation policy, not just to plant trees on the mountains, but to make a commercial forest complex with high economic efficiency so that it may serve to increase the residents' income……..". Accordingly, for over three years until 1979, a 2,000 ha commercial forest complex was completed at eighty-six locations.

This way, the First Ten-Year Forest Rehabilitation Plan was completed. Between 1973 and 1978, recording reforestation in 1.08 million ha, 2.9 billion trees planted, tree care in 4.18 million ha, and erosion control in 42,000ha, the ten-year targeted project was completed in six years. There is another thing to take special note of. The barren land around the country requiring urgent erosion control work reached 524,436 ha in 1960, the year previous to the military revolution, which was decreased in 1980 to 33,990 ha. [3] At last, President Park reforested 94 percent of the barren land during his eighteen years of reign. This is a battle with a clear victory, but it is senseless to wonder to whom the credit must go. The heroes of the victory were President Park, the Minister of Home Affairs, Kim Hyun-Ok, the Head of the Forest Service, Sohn Soo-Ik, all of the officials of the Forest Service, all of the local forest-related personnel, the farmers, and everyone. Any one group not fulfilling its share would have led to the failure of this battle.

As a forestry expert, the author analyzes the success factors of reforestation in the 1970s as follows:

1. President Park Chung-Hee: There was a strong will of the sovereign ruler on reforestation. Throughout his reign, he expressed continued interest, showing a strong drive, along with concrete instructions. In terms of personnel matters, he selected Sohn Soo-Ik, Head of the Forest Service, a person skilled in organized operations and had him remain in office for six years so that he might fulfill his duties according to his convictions. President Park also encouraged forestry officials in charge with a warm heart, and had the workers (businessmen, non-officials, or village people) feel the reward for their own reforestation work, keeping spirits high continuously. Officials in charge came to work devotedly when they realized the policy of their own making was consistently being carried out in the president's interest. Underlying such a successful reforestation were related officials who moved well-ordered, and the nation's passion was motivated by the national ruler's strong drive.

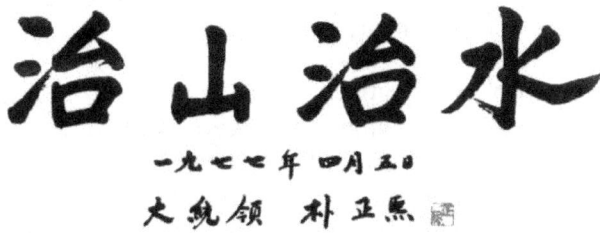

Photo 105. President Park emphasized that conservation of rivers and forests was one of the most important aims of the national administration all through the eighteen years of his reign (Chinese calligraphy of President Park in memory of the Arbor Day 1977)

2. Kim Hyun-Ok, Minister of Home Affairs: After setting the Saemaul project and reforestation project as the two major national policy tasks of the ministry, he assisted the president thoroughly. He had a great interest and enthusiasm in reforestation and didn't spare rigorous order and whole-heartedly supported the Forest Service (through disposal of forest offenses using police power, and installation of direct telephone lines, etc.) In particular, his new idea of "planted tree inspection system" resulted in the year-round monitoring and taking care of the tree seedlings planted in the spring, with eliminating any possibility of false record or report.

3. Sohn Soo-Ik, Head of the Forest Service: He exercised charismatic leadership for six years. He established an organic mutual aid system of related policy means and prepared a clear, efficient reforestation plan. He combined a thorough supervisory administration with strict oversight, visiting as many planting sites as possible to make the "planted tree inspection system" work properly and subsequently to increase the average survival rate of the planted trees to over 90 percent. He prepared an opportunity for extensive promotions of forestry officials and lifted their spirits by delivering the president's allowances to the lower organization.

4. Forestry officials: They exercised our people's unique diligence with full patriotic thinking in love of forests, with a continuous encouragement by the president. Together with pure hearts and working as a friend of nature, they felt satisfaction with their jobs, with great pride and rewards as reforestation advanced successfully later. They mostly remain alive in their advanced age in their seventies and eighties. It is believed that they stay healthy because they worked in the mountains, breathing clean air.

5. Village people's positive participation and Village Forestry Cooperative: At the beginning, they were mobilized in the form of forced labor, receiving the price of their labor in the form of relief grains. Getting out from under the burden of illegal gathering of fuel wood, they came to understand the necessity for establishing a fuel-wood forest in cooperation with one another and the government. They positively participated in the reforestation project through Village Forestry Cooperatives which undertook the decisive role in mobilizing labor for tree planting. They exercised the spirits of diligence, self-

reliance and cooperation through the Saemaul Movement, while earning some common income from village nursery and gradually understanding the benefits from dense forests.

6. Economic and social circumstances: At the beginning stage of forest rehabilitation, farm village food was in absolute short supply, incomes were low, but potential labor was rich, which facilitated mobilization of manpower. In the latter stage, both supply of substitute fuel in accordance with a rapid economic development and a decrease in farm population resulted in decreased gathering of leaf litter and fuel wood, which fundamentally reduced opportunities to damage the mountain forests.

Designation of Ardent Foresters

During the First Ten-Year Forest Rehabilitation Plan, there was an important project, although it may look unimportant; designation of an "ardent forester". The Forest Service decided that for the reforestation project, it was good to have non-government persons participate positively instead of relying 100 percent on the initiative of the government. Accordingly, the Forest Service made an institution that led reforestation among people who owned a large size (20 ha) mountain forest. The gist was that if an owner of a mountain forest was designated by the government as an "ardent forester", the policy fund was going to be supported for that person to plant trees easily. The policy fund was the money treated as blind money because of cheap interest and long periods of redemption. Also, in case there was no privately-owned forest, state forests would be leased in accordance with profit-share contracts with the income to be divided between the state and the person. The institution proposed that when cutting trees they had planted, 90 percent of the sales income could be taken by the ardent forester and the remaining 10 percent would be paid to the state.

Accordingly, forest owners formed what was called Korea Sivilculturist Association. Additionally, the Forest Service decided to designate the majority of these members as ardent foresters. In 1974, the first year of enforcing the institution, it designated 397 people from the whole country as ardent foresters. The idea could be criticized as wasteful, but it was a desperate plan. Among those "ardent foresters", however, there are persons who can touch our hearts. They are persons who left a great achievement in tree-planting well before they were designated as ardent foresters.

First, there is Lim Jong-Guk (1915–1987), who has been heralded as the reforestation king.[1] One day in 1956 when he was in early forties, he, after looking around a mountain owned by Kim Seong-Soo, a spiritual leader in Korea, at Deokjin-ri, Jangseong-gun, Jeonnam, was greatly impressed that only on this mountain there were sugi measuring more than both arm's span around and hinoki straight up, while surrounding mountains were bare ones then. He planted many trees in a total area of 569 ha for twenty years, including sugi and hinoki trees in the area of Jangseong-gun. When the spring drought was serious in 1968 and 1969, he helped young trees survive by digging a well in the stream, which touched village people, who helped him soon. The Forest Service inducted Lim Jong-Guk into the "Forest Hall of Fame" in 2001 following President Park Chung-Hee and Professor Hyun Shin-Kyu.

Photo 106. Mt. Chukryeong Hinoki forest at Jangseong, Jeonnam, established by Lim Jong-Guk is one of the most beautiful forests in Korea. Currently, the Forest Service is managing this forest for forest therapy.

The second ardent forester is Baekje Pharmaceutical president Kim Gi-Woon.[1] Residing in Mokpo City, Jeonnam, he had planted trees on an area of 1,000 ha in Gangjin-gun since 1968 when he was in his early thirties. He poured out profits from Baekje Pharmaceutical, a distributor of medical supplies, and Chodang Pharaceuticals, a manufacturer of medical supplies, into the Chodang forest in Gangjin toward his dream. He even planted trees, mobilizing as many as five hundred laborers a day, and on a stony mountain, he dug up stones and planted trees. In the beginning, young trees were buried under vigorous grasses, tangled with vines, and they died of drought. Later, among foreign tree species, he succeeded in planting loblolly pines, hinoki and tulip trees. In particular, tulip trees planted thirty years ago were found to be excellent in growth, which created an opportunity for the Forest Service to recommend it to the whole country as the most economical tree species for planting.

Photo 107. Tulip tree planted by Kim Gi-Woon has excellent enough growth and shape to have become a representative tree species recommended by the Forest Service (thirty-two years old, 72 cm in diameter, 27 m in height).

Another ardent forester came in the form of an enterprise rather than a person. Choi Jong-Hyeon, who had built SK Group into a global enterprise, founded "Seohae Development Co., Ltd," the current SK Forestry, Co. Ltd. for the purpose of encouraging learning. In the 1970s he planted trees in Yeongdong, Chungbuk, and Cheonan, Chungnam regions, sometimes hiring five hundred laborers a day. He planted 3.3 million trees, including white birch, walnut, and Manchurian walnut over a total of 4,000 ha. At the time of his death in 1998, President Choi, knowing that the total graveyards accounted for almost one percent of the total land area of Korea causing damage to mountain forests, left his dying wish that instead of being buried in a mountain forest, his body should be burned. After that, domestic funeral culture started to change by increasing the cremation rate of 30.3 percent in 1999 to 68 percent in 2012, providing an opportunity for a natural funeral. He was dedicated to the "Forest Hall of Fame" in April 2010.

Planted a Tree Even Several Hours before His Death

Now the First Ten-Year Forest Rehabilitation Plan, which was waged like a battle, came to an end. President Park Chung-Hee, the supreme commander of this battle, grandly took the honor of victory. However, the next year after the battle, he turned into a handful of ash returning to the place beside his much beloved trees, as did Admiral Lee Sun-Shin after wiping out the Japanese invaders. He realized the dream of reforestation of the country. During his life, he said many times that the forest rehabilitation project may seem to have generated no immediate profits, but it was the shortcut to making a beautiful country to live in. That was why he made a national policy project of forest rehabilitation and succeeded after all. Can there have been such a ruler in another country of the world?

He was always racking his brains to bring about forest rehabilitation as early as possible. Even on his way to local inspection, he felt sorry that reforestation had not been properly made in the area around the road and issued instant countermeasures. Deep down, he could have resented subordinate officials who weren't able to solve such small problems. However, President Park neither got angry nor irritated. He only taught, encouraged, and drove them. Really we had a nice gift, which was possible with good fortune for the country.

In the spring of 1979, to publicize the results of reforestation, the Forest Service opened the People's Tree Planting Exhibition Hall in Deoksu Palace in Seoul. Describing the history of mountain forests and relations between forest and man as a beautiful one of coexistence, it displayed the effect and efficacy a mountain forest can have on human life, kinds of trees, wooden products, forestry machinery, etc. Typical slogans exhibited here include the following:

"Tree-planting, strong country; Tree-cut, ruined country!"

"Rivers, mountains, and country flourished by growing trees!"

"Planting trees by the whole nation, making the green land!"

"One tree per person, thirty million trees, forest reclamation and economic reconstruction!"

Photo 108. After completing the First Ten-Year Forest Rehabilitation plan four years early, the People's Tree Planting Exhibition Hall was established to commemorate it (Deoksu Palace, March 31, 1979).

In 1979, the "Second Ten-Year Forest Rehabilitation Plan (1979–1988) started. This second plan included a long-term plan for using mountain areas, establishing commercial forest complexes, developing native woody species, expanding foreign forest resources, and continuing erosion-control project. In particular, a forest land-use classification survey was enforced to allow the management of mountain areas across the country. Forests were divided into either reserve forests or non-reserve forests in order to prevent excessive development of and damage to mountain forests. Establishing large-complex commercial forests was proposed for 400,000 ha and to diversify planting tree species. The ten major planting tree species in the first plan were expanded into twenty-one species in the second plan.

At last the Second Ten-Year Forest Rehabilitation Plan was completed in 1987, one year earlier than scheduled, planting a total of 1.92 billion trees on 966 thousand ha of mountain land. With the successful completion of the First (1973-1978) and the Second (1979-1987) Ten-Year Forest Rehabilitation Plans, in which a total of 4.88 billion trees on 2.05 million ha were planted, the mountains in the whole country were fully clothed in green. The next year the Olympic Games were held and finished successfully.

In the testimony (transcript) at the Park Chung-Hee Memorial Society, Kim Yeon-Pyo, the former Vice Head of the Forest Service, was carried away with emotion, saying, "After the World War II, Korea is the only country on earth that has been successful in manually reforesting the entire country, which had been completely devastated for a century."

On December 27, 1978, Park was inaugurated as the ninth president, and at the time, per capita GNP was $1,396. The next year, on October 26, 1979, President Park died at the age of sixty-two. The president performed a commemorative tree planting on the day of his death, which was his last planting. After the opening ceremony of the Sapgyocheon sea wall, he attended the ceremony for completion of the KBS relay towers in Dangjin, Chungnam, and planted a tree for commemoration. Heaven ordained that President Park would plant a tree even on the day of his death so that the people might remember his love of trees.

Chapter 20. Reforestation of the Country More Precious Than Economic Development

The Only Developing Country with Success in Forest Reclamation

Successful forest reclamation executed in the 1970s allowed Korea to have dense forests. The FAO (Food and Agriculture Organization), a UN agency based in Rome, sent out specialists to investigate Korea's tree-planting project. In 1982, through an official report[33], the FAO extolled Korea's forest reclamation project, saying, "The Republic of Korea is the only developing country in the world that has succeeded in reforestation since the Second World War." The FAO also indicated that together with West Germany, the United Kingdom, and New Zealand, Korea was among the four major successful countries in reforestation. In particular, Korea's designation has a special meaning because it was completely reforested in a short period after a longtime desolate state of mountains and forests on a nationwide scale. This must be the first-ever case of this kind of success on earth.

While Kim Chung-Yum, the Presidential Chief of Staff, was the Korean ambassador to Japan after President Park's death, Hukuda Dakeo, the former Japanese premier, cherished the memory of President Park saying, "From the days of Japanese colonialism, Korea was associated with bare mountains. It is difficult to restore mountains and forests once they are destroyed. Despite that, President Park has succeeded in a complete reforestation of the country in less than twenty years of his reign. It is a more difficult and more valuable feat than his achievement of brilliant economic development, such as high growth, increased exports, and the heavy chemical industry." [9]

William Gleysteen was the US ambassador to Korea who persuaded US President Jimmy Carter, who was visiting Korea in 1979, to revoke his earlier election promise to withdraw the US Army from Korea. After leaving the post of ambassador, he commented that President Park was "an indigenous Korean who never forgot about the place he was born and farm people."

In 2006, Lester Brown, Director of the US World Policy Institute, wrote in his book <*Plan B 2.0: Rescuing a Planet Under Stress and a Civilization in Trouble*>, "South Korea is in many ways a reforestation model for the rest of the world……. It was gratifying for me to see the luxuriant stand of trees on mountains that a generation ago were bare. We can reforest the earth."

Photo 109. President Park had not confirmed the completion of the forest reclamation when he died in 1979. Instead, President Noh Tae-Woo left his own writing in commemoration (April 5, 1992, Garden of Gwangneung Korea National Arboretum)

Park Ji-Man, President Park's son, said in an interview with Jo Gap-Je, "My father was a man who loved living creatures. He liked a tree, a flower, and a puppy so much. I find there is no writing about my father from that aspect."[5] Jo Gap-Je writes,

"I think that his success in forest reclamation is not due to his sense of obligation, but is the result of his love of forest and trees....... In his diary, we can find so many sentimental expressions about fallen leaves, flowers, trees, clouds, etc. It makes us feel his warm affection and concern for little things. His diary is so pure that it is like that of an elementary school student, not a person in power. On the day for a farm village inspection, Park Chung-Hee seemed to be on top of the world, like a boy going on a picnic. On this day, too, he received and put on his suit humming some song and moving his shoulders up and down." [5]

According to his elder daughter Park Geun-Hye who became the eighteenth president of Korea in 2013, President Park wanted to prepare a small forest land for his family after resigning from the Blue House and live silently taking care of trees. Her mother's wish was even stronger. Her mother, the First Lady, said she wished to buy a small parcel of land and live by farming and growing trees. But while sharing this topic with the president several times, they worried greatly about the public misunderstanding in relation to buying land. [2]

Since President Park's death, many things that enable one to conjecture about his general life philosophy have become known.[5] On October 26, 1979, after being shot by one of his aides, President Park was transported to an army hospital nearby. Those attending to him saw that he wore a cheap, old watch on his wrist, a neck-tie pin with gilt coming off, and a worn-out belt on his pants. Right after his death, people discovered in President Park's bedroom a red brick in the water tank of the restroom toilet put in by the president in private. A similar brick was also found in the president's exclusive restroom at his office on the first floor, which indicated he tried to save water in his daily life.

To save electricity, the president didn't turn on the air conditioner in the Blue House, but opened the window. So President Park had to catch the flies coming in with a fly flap. One day, it was so hot that the secretaries only circulated the air without turning on the air conditioner. President Park told Geun-Hye, his daughter, at the dinner table, "Those bastards turned on the air conditioner. Didn't they think I would know when it suddenly got cool? Tell them never to turn it on from now on."

Bae Jin-Seong, reporter for *Monthly Chosun*, writes, "Even after he became president, President Park didn't seek any interests or honor for his own sake, but appeared to be the picture of devotion to the national interest. This quality drew the devotion of his men, as some of his aides (Kim Chung-Yum, Presidential Chief of Staff) said, "It was the greatest reward as a man to meet the great president and work for him and the country."[22]

Korea: Miracle in the Twentieth Century

On August 15, 2005, marking the sixtieth anniversary of the national Liberation, the press and every organization published the diverse poll results on historical persons (cited from President Park Chung-Hee Memorial Society Newsletter No. 5).[6] According to this, President Park overwhelmed other politicians in all categories with a significant difference between first and second place.

■ *HanKook Ilbo* **Daily News**

• *The most influential politician*

1st Park Chung-Hee (71.9 %), 2nd Kim Dae-Jung (26.5 %), 3rd (Jeon Du-Hwan (11.0 %)

• *The most competent president*

1st Park Chung-Hee (72.4 %), 2nd Kim Dae-Jung (18.4 %), 3rd Jeon Du-Hwan (1.6 %)

■ **KBS**

• *The greatest president in history*

1st Park Chung-Hee (55.2 %), 2nd Kim Dae-Jung (17.2 %), 3rd Rhee Syng-Man (2.5 %)

■ **College Students' Internet Newspaper '*To You*'**

• *The most excellent president in history*

1st Park Chung-Hee (46.7 %), 2nd Kim Dae-Jung (20.5 %), 3rd No Mu-Hyeon (4.2 %)

Photo 110. Planting first fast-growing trees in the spirit of Saemaul, using the rich labor of the farm villages in the 1970s was the secret of success in forest reclamation.

One foreign reporter who has watched Korea's modern history said, "Korea has not simply developed but skyrocketed." Peter F. Drucker (1909 – 2005), well known to our country as a godfather to the world's business administration said, "I would say that the most amazing among the results human kind has accomplished since the Second World War is South Korea."[2]

In August 2010, *Newsweek*, a US weekly magazine, announced the rankings of the best countries of the world. Considering education, health, living environment, economic potential, and political stability, the first three in order were Finland, Switzerland, Sweden, and Korea ranked fifteenth. In the East, only Japan (ninth) and Korea belonged to the upper-ranking group. UNDP (Development Programme) is trying to rank countries of the world based on the HDI (Human Development Index) which is a composite statistic of life expectancy, education, and income. The 2011 Human Development Report by the UNDP showed that Norway ranked first and South Korea ranked fifteenth in the world in human development. It is widely known that Korea has reached a point comparable to advanced countries in its economy, trade size, and quality of life. Who built the foundation? The author believes it was President Park who, with a keen insight ahead of his own time, encouraged the people and planted many trees.

Talks about President Park's merits and demerits necessarily involve his "push" policy. In fact, during his eighteen years of reign, Park Chung-Hee issued innumerable directives orally or with his signature. They are all one-sided directives, of course. However, according to the "instruction statement" remaining in Daejeon Government's Archives, President Park didn't use the word "reform" a single time. That is, it was a principle of rule that actions spoke louder than words. He didn't use the language but did instigate a great reform and progress in history.

It is obvious why President Park had to push everything forward. On November 25, 1969, in an administrative policy speech, he said "We should work while others are resting; we should run while others are walking." President Park's Promethean thoughts and "Quick, quick" attitude were ideas very compatible with the speedy information society we have now. If we had not hurried economic development and technical improvement before other countries had a chance to join the queue for competition, it would not be possible for us, a later starter, to beat China or other southeast countries in fierce international competition as we do in these days.

Photo 111. Of many species planted for timber at that time, Norway spruce has been successful with a straight trunk.

The same goes for forest reclamation. It would have been a totally impossible project with working conditions or economic circumstances nowadays if we had not hurried to push forward then. Hurried, President Park completed forest reclamation. He restored picturesque rivers and mountains. Especially as time goes on, his resolution to set forest reclamation as a top priority shines out. Some may think that the plan to hurry failed to create a more useful commercial forest, but looking back now, his decision is considered to have been right.

In the spring of 1977, in a meeting with reporters, President Park said, "I have not worked for the popularity of this time but I've always worked keeping in mind how future historians will record my agenda."[6] History cannot be measured by today's ruler. Though under a warlike Yushin system, he pushed forward forest reclamation by force, and he managed his role as "benevolent dictator" for restoring the scenic beauty unselfishly, adhering to a creed of upright living.

Prepared a Basis for "Green Growth"

It has been over thirty years since President Park died. These days it is impossible to expand the reforestation project because of a decrease in the farming population, aging, high personnel expenses, and a lack of eagerness to participate or a cooperative spirit. Besides, recent public sentiment that stresses the importance of environmental protection has made large-scale felling and tree species replacement almost impossible. Therefore, if we had not completed the forest reclamation in an early period when there was plentiful and cheap labor and a positive response from farmers to overcome their hunger, the argument could be made that Korea would not have surmounted the problem of desolate mountains and forests. In addition, if President Park had not completed the First Ten-Year Forest Rehabilitation Plan in six years, the plan may not have been completed. And it is very likely that forest reclamation might not have been properly finished, considering that he died the next year.

Of course, there is a problem. Together, the one-sided drive for forest reclamation and the strong sense of forest protection possessed by President Park have brought on the following two dysfunctions. That is, forest reclamation is a national project, so it can be achieved without the people's voluntary participation. Second, because of the generally accepted idea that planting is a social good and cutting is a social evil, even when one plants a tree in his land, he cannot cut it as he wishes. This has caused an atmosphere of avoiding forest investment among the people.

Photo 112. Dense forest is a necessary and sufficient condition for a rich farm village.

It is also true that there is criticism against having planted only noncommercial trees. However, the author holds the following positive opinions on the trees species planted. Italian poplar was planted by village people in cooperation on the river-bank that could not be used for farming. Since it was a fast-growing tree, it gave great help to an early stage of reforestation. Being able to harvest it in fifteen years greatly contributed to the income of farmers, while the poplar scholarship has been made to open the way for model students to go on to upper-class school, which has fulfilled its role sufficiently.

Black locust, which changes inert nitrogen gas in the air into organic nitrogen fertilizer, is a soil-improving tree species on infertile land. Its wood was used for fuel, solving the problem of shortage of fuel wood in poor farmers. Its timber was used to build ox carts. These days, being the hardest and most durable wood among timbers harvested from the forest care project, it is being widely used for benches on the mountain paths. The black locust wood is very durable for use outdoors in the weather. That is, the wood requires no preservative treatment for construction of a playpen, a pergola for climbing plants or a pavilion in traditional gardens. In addition, it is a honey-producing plant on which apiarists depend for 70 percent of their income. Their bees are pollinating the flowers in both orchards and polyethylene vinyl houses throughout the whole country. For reforestation in the desolate mountains of North Korea now, there is no other alternative but to plant black locust in order to prevent soil erosion, to supply fuel wood, and to improve soil fertility as we have experienced with the black locust in South Korea.

Alder is a soil-improving tree that fertilizes the soil as the black locust does, and it has built the basis of the dense forest we have now. Its wood is used for fuel wood and manufactured for ritual vessels. Pitch pine, which grows well in barren forest soil like we have in Korea, was planted for erosion control and the fuel-wood forest because it produces new shoots easily from the trunk base after harvesting. It has recently been used for stabilizing both riverbanks and earth in erosion-control project, and is also used for medium-density fiberboard (MDF). The Hyun poplar (*Populus alba* x *glandulosa*) was excellent as a roadside tree and is the only "poplar for mountain slopes" that can be planted in soil depleted of moisture and nutrients. It also has white bark, which adds scenic beauty. These days it is planted as a tree for purifying polluted soil in the vicinity of a cattle shed.

Although President Park has died, our economy continued rapid growth. At the end of 1977, its total exports exceeded $10 billion and per capital GNP in 1979 was $1,644. But in 2004, a quarter century after park's death, total exports increased to $250 billion, of which the portion occupied by the heavy chemical industry products was $208 billion. In 2008, the country achieved exports of $400 billion and exceeded $500 billion in 2010. It makes us realize how significantly the heavy chemical industry, driven by President Park, has affected our economy. In memory of his great achievements, the Korean government subsidized budget for building the President Park Chung-Hee Memorials and Library which was completed in February 2012 in Sangam-dong, Mapo-gu, Seoul.

Photo 113. Achieving $10 billion of exports within his period of reign rendered an indirect help in forest reclamation, too, by substituting forest fuel (December 22, 1977, in Gwanghwamun, Seoul, in memory of exporting $10 billion).

On November 25, 2009, Korea entered the Development Assistance Committee (DAC) under OECD as the twenty-fourth member state. The foreign media reported that Korea was the only case of having transformed from a supported into a supporting country. In particular, we forestry persons take pride in building the foundation for the "green growth" the Korean government has recently been seeking, believing that President Park's foresight and will toward forest reclamation has underlain such success.

Photo 114. President Park Chung-Hee Memorials and Library was completed in February 2012 in Sangam-dong, Mapo-gu, Seoul.

Presented to the Forest Hall of Fame

On April 5, 2001, the fifty-sixth Arbor Day event was the twenty-second since President Park's death. On the event of this day, there was one unusual event. It was to dedicate President Park to the "Forest Hall of Fame". To honor those who have greatly contributed to forest reclamation, the government built the "Forest Hall of Fame" in Gwangneung Forest Museum, Gyeonggi-do. Here President Park Chung-Hee was dedicated along with Dr. Hyun Sin-Kyu, to commemorate his contributions to forest reclamation. Indeed, President Park had enormous energy for forest reclamation. His continuous interest was expressed by endless instructions for reforestation during many government meetings such as cabinet meetings, economy-related minister's meetings, governor's meetings, and local inspection meetings.

Photo 115. On April 5, 2001, the Forest Service dedicated President Park to the "Forest Hall of Fame" in recognition of his achievements in forest reclamation (Garden of Korea National Arboretum, Gwangneung, Gyeonggi-do).

As introduced earlier, Lester Brown, Director of the World Policy Institute, said in 2006 that Korea's forest reclamation is a model for the world. The forest reclamation in a developing country seems to be more difficult than economic development. Korea is acting as a model for other countries in both forest reclamation and economic development. Now Korea is asserting itself as the greatest example of successful reforestation and environment protection in the world, and also positively participates in the desertification prevention project in East Asian region, such as China, Mongolia, and Myanmar. Among methods of preventing global warming, the two most positive are reducing emissions of carbon dioxide and forest reclamation, the latter of which is the part that Korea is taking initiative in and giving hope to developing countries.

Epilogue:

From Incompletion to Completion

A dense forest is national wealth itself and the road to becoming an advanced country. Countries in the world that are good to live in have dense forests without exception, while their national character is worth imitating because the people love forests. With the two successive ten-year reforestation plans from 1973 to 1987, Korean government planted a total of 4.88 billion trees on 2.05 million ha of barren land. President Park Chung-Hee drove with strong will the forest rehabilitation project during his entire period of reign, and later received commendation for the twentieth-century miracle of developing the country on a global scale.

President Park divided reforestation of the country into two stages. The first stage focused on covering bare mountains that poured out earth, as well as solving the fuel-wood problem for the whole population. Until entering the 1960s, most households of the country used wood or charcoal for cooking and heating material. For supplying fuel wood, he planted fast-growing trees first and quickly reforested the desolate land by planting soil-improving trees. Though at that time there was considerable opposition to fast-growing trees, the author, as an expert in forestry, considers that President Park's decision was right. By having an "early-stage completion" policy of tree-planting, he set up the First Ten-Year Forest Rehabilitation Plan in 1973 and solved the urgent problem of fuel wood while preparing a basis for planting a better tree species by improving the barren land. Of course, erosion control and slash-and-burn farming regulation projects succeeded. North Korea, which has neglected its forests, is still helpless against damage from drought, flood, and the destruction of rice paddies and dry fields caused by landslides. On the other hand, South Korea has accomplished self-sufficiency of rice by having a stable water supply, has introduced a national park system and greenbelt system in an effort to seek a balance between conservation and development of the whole country, and has restored the picturesque rivers and mountains.

President Park's second stage was a conversion of simple forests to diversified forests. The second stage reforestation, represented by the Second Ten-Year Forest Rehabilitation Plan, began in 1979 and included a long-term forest land-use plan, the establishment of commercial forest, the development of both local tree species and oversea forest resources. However, President Park died on October 26, leaving an uncompleted symphony.

These days, the Forest Service's intention to cut down trees having no economic value and to renew the tree species is meeting resistance. Perhaps because of the great emphasis on forest protection of bare mountains in the past, our people tend to have a wrong viewpoint on trees and forests after the forest has become dense. Among the people there is a perception that cutting trees is all bad and an act of destroying the environment. It is incomprehensible that while all the nation is consuming timbers and paper as much as they want, the people emphasize only forest function of preserving environment.

It is obvious that currently, the forest resources of our country are environmental resources. However, they should not end with environmental resources. It is time that we need to transform forest resources into "environmental resources with economic efficiency". Circumstances are ripe for establishing commercial forests because the mountain soil has been improved and our country depends too much on the imported timbers.

Domestic circumstances of timber supply are very bad. We imported 84 percent of domestic timber requirements in 2012, and have poor prospects for self-sufficiency of timber in the future. Expecting a future global shortage of timber, we need to build up our timber resources on artificial plantations. But as of 2009, the total area of artificial forests is only 1.71 million ha, which accounts for only 27 percent of the total forest area. Although the Forest Service is reforesting around 20,000 ha each year, amounts to only one eighth of the area in President Park's days. Instead, on the basis of creating jobs, the government is executing the "Forest Care Project" for natural forests. It amounts to 300 to 400 thousand ha annually, which is not a small area. But they are natural forests that have declined in the past, and most trees have crooked stems with less value as timber.

What forest policy should Korea unfold in the future to complete the unfinished tune? The answer is to build up economic resources of the forest. In a shortage of underground resources, we should secure ground resources sufficiently to survive international competition. First, the government should gradually purchase the private forests whose owners do not invest in them or have the right of management consigned to the government to manage them intensively. We should also actively reforest abandoned agricultural land at the foot of the mountains. In addition, we should plant tree species with high photosynthetic rates and fast growth to prevent global warming and to foster timber resources. As advanced forest countries do, we should keep transforming natural forests with low productivity into artificial forests with high productivity using improved seed at this time.

Tree species suited for this purpose have already been secured. The tulip tree is an introduced tree species with its excellence proved recently. For the southern region, pitch-lolly pine, Sugi and Hinoki have high value as timber, while for northern part, Korean white pine and larch do. Though oak and red pine are rather slow in growth, they need to be planted with further improvement because they are native species growing around the country. Black locust is a tree species well worth planting in narrow spaces for timber use after developing new varieties with straight stems as Hungary in Europe is currently doing.

Marking the twenty-first century, we should maximize diverse functions of the forest. That is, our forests in the future should meet the various functions at the same time, such as production of timber and forest by-products, supply of bio-energy [economic function], conservation of the country, supply of clean water, air purification and prevention of global warming [environmental function], preservation of biodiversity and protection of wildlife [ecological function], and forest recreation and forest therapy [health and recuperative function]. It is the very path of transforming incompleteness into completeness, which is not so difficult if people develop an understanding of the various functions of forests.

For future forestry, diverse ideas have now been presented. The government may become a direct agent of such forest management, but having an enterprise manage the forest according to market principles can improve efficiency even more. If government promotes a large forest complex by integrating the rights of management while leaving ownership of private forests intact, it could rather develop into an industry with economic efficiency.

President Park has provided us an excellent gift of completed conservation of rivers and forests. Thanks to him, we have freed ourselves from hunger and come to enjoy a beautiful natural environment, laying a foundation for incumbent President Lee Myung-Bak to clarify in 2008 "green growth" to the world, marking the sixtieth anniversary of the government establishment.

However, it is not right for us to be content with our accomplishments. If we are content with the current state, our descendants with neither underground nor ground resources will have to repeat a vicious cycle of exporting something manufactured by the sweat of their brow and importing crude oil and even timber with that money. So how can we return President Park's exertion of the mind and be estimated by offspring as a wise ancestor? We can do so by converting the current forest into both beautiful and rich ground resources to create national wealth as advanced countries do.

References

1. Korea Forest Service. 2007. Korean Forests: A World-Wide Known Miracle. Korea Forestry Weekly News (Editor). 992p.

2. Kim, In Man. 2008. Park Chung Hee: From Anecdotes to Myths. Seorim Munhwa Publ. Seoul, Korea. 334p.

3. Korea Forest Service. 2007. The Hundred-Year History of Korea Erosion Control (1907-2007). Korea Forest Service. 838p.

4. Jo, Gab Je. 2007. Park Chung Hee Vol. 1-13. Jogabje.Com. Publ. Seoul, Korea.

5. Jo, Gab Je. 2009. The Decisive Moments of Park Chung Hee. Gyiparang Publ. Seoul, Korea. 806p.

6. President Park Chung Hee Memorial Society. 2013. Internet Homepage. http://516.co.kr

7. Im, Il Je. 2007. Recollection of a great achievement on afforestation. President Park Chung Hee Memorial Society Report No.14.

8. Kim, Hyung Kook. 2009. Afforestation by President Park Chung Hee. President Park Chung Hee Memorial Society Report No. 19.

9. Kim, Chung-Yum. 2011. From Despair to Hope: Economic Policymaking in Korea 1945-1979. Korea Development Institute, Seoul, Korea. 582p.

10. Park, Jin Hwan. 2005. Economic Modernization and New Village Movement in Korea. President Park Chung Hee Memorial Society, Seoul, Korea. 256p.

11. Sohn, Soo Ik. 2006. Contribution of President Park Chung Hee to world forestry policy: President Park and Afforestation. President Park Chung Hee Memorial Society Report No. 7.

12. Oh, Whee Young. 2000. Hidden stories on Korean modern landscape architecture(1)-(5). Environment and Landscape Architecture. No. 141- 145.

13. Park, In Je. 2002. A study on transition in the city parks in Seoul. Ph. D. Thesis of Sangmyung University. Seoul, Korea.

14. Pae, Jeong-Hann. 2003. Park Chung-Hee's thoughts on landscape architecture. Journal of Korean Institute of Landscape Architecture. 31(4): 13-24.

15. Kim, Chung-Yum. 1997. Oh! Park Chung Hee. Joongang M & B. Seoul, Korea. 367p.

16. Ahn, Hyo Bin. 1977. A Close Look to President Park Chung Hee. Hyumun Publ. Seoul, Korea.

17. Kim, Seong Jin. 2006. Speaking about Park Chung Hee. Life and Dream. Seoul, Korea. 308p.

18. O, Won-Chul. 2009. The Korea Story: President Park Jung-hee's Leadership and the Korean Industrial Revolution. Wisdom Tree Publisher, Seoul, Korea. 807p.

19. Jeong, Je Hun. 2000. My way and my life: Eradication of Japanese works and establishment of new landscape architecture for cultural heritage. Environment and Landscape Architecture. 144: 36-39.

20. Jeong, Je Kyung. 1992. A Hero Park Chung Hee. Jipmundang, Seoul, Korea. 335p.

21. Kim, Yeon Pyo. 1999. A testimony on half century agricultural policy: Transfer and return of Korea Forest Service. In Half Century History

of Korea Agricultural Policy. Vol. 3. 415-431. Korea Rural Economic Institute, Seoul, Korea.

22. Bae, Jin Seong. 2003. Government live voice document on heroic CEO Park Chung Hee. Monthly Chosun, June Issue, 2003.

23. Lee, Kyung Joon. 2006. A Pioneer Who Planted Future in Forest. Seoul National University Press, Seoul, Korea. 321p.

24. Bae, Cheong. 2006. Greenbelt policy of President Park Chung Hee in view of international comparison. President Park Chung Hee Memorial Society Report No. 8.

25. Ryu, Tae Young. 2005. President Park Chung Hee and his leadership. President Park Chung Hee Memorial Society Report No. 3.

26. Ko, Byung Woo. 2006. Turning point from poverty in Korean history: From Farmer and Fisherman Income-Boosting Program to New Village Movement. President Park Chung Hee Memorial Society Report No. 9.

27. Kim, Du Young. 1990. A close look into man Park Chung Hee. Monthly Chosun, December Issue, 1990. 424 - 447.

28. Lee, Geon Young. 1996. Victory of the Defeated. Jinmyung Munhwasa, Seoul, Korea. 410p.

29. Government Publication. 1973. Presidential Directions: Annual Visit to Ministries in 1973 (Ministry of Home Affairs). The Office of Presidential Secretary.

30. Park, Kee Ju. 2010. Twilight of the empire: We 100 years ago (Series 99). Chosun Daily News. January 15, 2010. Seoul, Korea.

31. Lee, Jong Beom. 1994. Administrative Officials in the Period of Turnover: Korean Style Leaders. Nanam Publ., Seoul, Korea. 367p.

32. Gyeongsangbuk-do. 1999. The Hundred Year History of Erosion Control in Gyeongbuk. Gyeongsangbuk-do Province. 1004p.

33. Food and Agriculture Organization. 1982. Village Forestry Development in the Republic of Korea. A case Study. Forestry for local community development programme (GCP/INT/347/SWE). Rome, Italy. 104p.

About the Author

Professor Emeritus, Dr. LEE Kyung-Joon graduated from the Department of Forestry, Seoul National University, South Korea and studied at the University of Wisconsin, Madison for the M. S. and the University of Florida, Gainesville, USA for the Ph. D. After some years of research at the Institute of Forest Genetics, Korea, he served for twenty-five years as a professor at the Department of Forest Sciences, Seoul National University. He founded the University Plant Clinic, served as a director for the Clinic, and retired from the university in 2010.

He was the President of Korea Forest Society, and a Committee Member of Cultural Heritage in Cultural Heritage Administration. He has written and co-authored several books on forestry and trees, which include "Tree Physiology" and "Maintenance of Landscape Trees". He also wrote books in Korean on the history of Korean forestry focused on forest rehabilitation which included *A Pioneer Who Planted Future in Forests* and *A miracle Made by Park Chung-Hee: From Bald to Dense Forests*.

e-mail: fraxinus19@gmail.com